Bright Light

A Lifetime of Seeing God at Work

"I have known Harold Burchett for more than thirty years, as friend and colleague, but I find here dozens and dozens of stories I never heard before. Incredible stories, many hard to believe, but impacting me powerfully. Harold is a master storyteller, so I'm delighted to have these insights into his inner-life journey, many told here for the first time. A riveting account! Thank you, Harold, for sharing."

—J. Robertson McQuilkin, former president (1968-90) of Columbia International University

"*Bright Light*, a new book by Harold Burchett, is aptly titled. It brings to mind the disciples' experience on the Mount of Transfiguration, where they saw the bright glory of God in his beloved Son, Jesus. Harold here shares story after story of times he himself has witnessed God answering specific prayers—in his own life, in his public preaching, and in his personal interactions with needy people. Brightness indeed! And Harold's conclusion points the way toward brightness for *every* disciple of Christ: 'God still works powerfully in our day in answer to prayer' (from the preface)."

—Richard A. Peters, former pastor and missionary; member of Harold's first church (Nashua, N.H.)

"Dr. Harold Burchett is a man who *knows* God. As a spiritual grandson, I have come to know Harold personally in these last few years and have been changed. He is a man who loves the Lord Jesus and to whom the Lord has given unusual and profound insight. I commend this book (and his other writings) to teach you and give you encouragement and hope (Rom. 15:4)."

—Chap Bettis, elder/pastor (1987-2012) of New Covenant Christian Fellowship, Attleboro, Mass.; executive director of The Apollos Project, http://theapollosproject.com

"As I read through this short telling of a very remarkable man's life, I was struck by how many stories Harold Burchett chose *not* to include. . . . Harold's remarkable life has been characterized by believing prayer offered up to God and, again and again, by breakthrough answers granted by God. His life has also been marked by deep, penetrating ministry to others through a sort of "spiritual soul surgery" marked by the wise use of Scripture, gospel grace, and the personal ministry of the Holy Spirit. While many pray for great revivals from on high, Harold has been used of God to usher in life-changing revival to scores of people— one person at a time. And the spiritual fruit often seems to last to the third and the fourth generation! May this too-short autobiography stir many to turn to God in prayer with fresh hope and expectancy."

—Tim Kerr, pastor, Sovereign Grace Church Toronto

Other books by Harold Burchett:

People Helping People: How Every Christian Can Counsel
(Chicago: Moody Press, 1979; repr., 2015)
Spiritual Life Studies: A Manual for Personal Edification
(published by the author, 1980; 3rd, expanded ed., 2015)
Healing for the Church: New Life for You and Your Church
(published by the author, 1989; 2nd, expanded ed., 2015)
Last Light: Staying True through the Darkness of Alzheimer's
(Colorado Springs: NavPress, 2002; expanded ed., 2015)
Bringing Christ Back: Restoring Christ's Powerful Presence
(Bringing Christ Back Ministries, 2006; 2nd ed., 2015)
Wisdom Words (Bringing Christ Back Ministries, 2008; repr.,
2015)

Books, in e-book and print-on-demand formats, can be ordered
from the author's website (bcbministries.com) and from
Amazon.com.

Bright Light

A Lifetime of Seeing God at Work

Harold Ewing Burchett

Bringing Back Christ Ministries
www.bcbministries.com

Published 2013 by
Bringing Christ Back Ministries
www.bcbministries.com

ISBN: 978-0-9898179-0-5

Printed in the United States of America

The Scripture quotations in this publication are taken from the *Holy Bible, New International Version*, copyright © 1973, 1978, 1984 by the International Bible Society. Used by permission of Zondervan Bible Publishers.

Contents

Foreword

"Taste and see that the LORD is good; blessed is the man who takes refuge in him" (Ps.34:8). These words, penned by Israel's King David 3,000 years ago, may be the best single-sentence commentary on the life of Harold Ewing Burchett, whose memoirs appear here.

At a very young age, Harold received a loving introduction to this Lord from his parents and extended family. He was taught, and he himself sought, to find his refuge only in the Lord God and in his Son, Jesus Christ. Step by step, from early beginnings all the way now to his late eighties, this young sapling continued in a life-alignment with God. Along the way, a sturdy oak took shape and matured, a product both of Harold's chosen life direction and of the same Spirit who coauthored David's words.

But what kind of goodness does the Lord have to offer? And what sort of blessing might a person expect who "takes refuge" in God? I think Harold would answer, "You might be surprised!" As a youngster, Harold had no idea that he would experience blessings as a teenager on a battleship locked in combat in the South Pacific, or in his twenties as an itinerant preacher in the Canadian Maritimes witnessing remarkable revival stirrings, or in the last two decades of his first marriage caring at home for a wife with Alzheimer's—or that even one night, with loaded rifle, he would be chasing a kidnapper in his neighborhood! In all these settings and many more, as these pages reveal, Harold tasted and saw goodness and blessing that has every mark of a living God who, even in this modern/postmodern era, still stands by his ancient words.

What guidelines would Harold pass on to readers from a lifetime full of remarkable experiences? One is, "Stay everlastingly in prayer." Another is, Know that "God's eye is on the little ones, the weak ones, not the strong movers and shakers." My advice, therefore, is to take these stories and lessons, not so much shining a spotlight backward on Harold's life as pointing the way forward for every single one of us—especially if we feel ordinary or unqualified—helping us to believe that God is really real, and that he's good!

I have known Harold, as pastor and friend, since 1973. Most recently, we have been members together of the New Covenant Christian Fellowship, in Attleboro, Massachusetts. Here, during a recent search for a full-time elder/pastor, Harold stepped into the pulpit and, week by week, month by month, taught and counseled us about serving the God he knows and has witnessed in action all these years. Two observations: Harold really banks on prayer. And he knows deep down that God is loving and trustworthy. I suspect that these convictions are just the bedrock we need for revival in our day, in our world.

CRAIG A. NOLL, editor
Wm. B. Eerdmans Publishing Co.

Preface

Numbers of stories I am about to relate have been kept untold for many years because some of the happenings will seem marvelous and even hard to believe; I am a reluctant writer. In recent years, however, I have more and more felt a constraint to share these experiences. After counseling with trusted friends for their advice, I am proceeding. May glory come to God who has shown his mercy to me.

Looking back over more than eighty years of seeing God work, I have recalled times of wonderful spiritual revival, public and private—but also more than one occasion when my life was threatened. And in the course of seeking to minister to others, God has granted me very precious insights into the Christian life. Through it all, I can see now that God has employed several protective barriers to guard me from possible spiritual failure and disaster:

1. All through my maturing years I was kept from gaining money. Here was a responsibility I did not have!
2. I was kept from public notice—a burden I did not bear.
3. In my older years I was given an ongoing lock-in with my wife's Alzheimer's Disease. This weakening

seclusion promoted spiritual insight and strength. I did not attain it all, but my way was more hedged in and directed toward God's goal.

My apology for writing so much about my own experiences? Mainly it's this: these pages are intended to show what God did to, in, and for one servant of his, not what that servant did. Readers of these pages will, I think, have only two possible conclusions: either I am spinning some tall tales, or else God still works powerfully in our day in answer to prayer.

Here I wish to express my gratitude to Craig Noll for help given along the way. First, he and his wife, Anne, kindly listened to my vision for this book and encouraged me to proceed. Then, once the writing started, Craig gave valuable assistance at every turn in the editorial process. Finally, as a brother in Christ, he and I prayed and worked together through the many challenges that arose in the course of preparing this text for publication.

Warmest thanks to my wife, Cheryl, for her loving support, which included hours at the computer patiently recording my dictation.

Chronology

August 2, 1924: Harold Ewing Burchett is born to Randall Ewing Burchett and Mary Smith Burchett, natives of Clarksville, Tenn. Harold's siblings are Charles (1923-2008) and Virginia (1930-).

spring 1941: Harold begins work as a news reporter.

November 1943: Harold enlists in the Navy, takes basic training in San Diego, and on January 13, 1944, sets sail for Hawaii on the USS *Hopewell,* a destroyer serving as a forward picket ship in the Seventh Fleet.

January–September 1944: The *Hopewell* takes part in the invasion of the Marshall Islands, including the Battle of Kwajalein, and supports the landings at Aitape and at Hollandia of Western New Guinea, as well as other actions prior to the Philippines campaign.

January 1945: Harold receives a rare one-man transfer from the war zone back to the States for advanced training in electronics. After visiting his parents in Clarksville, he reports to naval schools in Chicago, ending at Navy Pier, renowned for its laboratories in radar and sonar. He is assigned to a destroyer escort in Boston, but the war ends, and he does not go back to sea.

March 9, 1946: Harold is discharged from the Navy in Boston.

April 1946: After resting a couple of months at home in Clarksville,

Harold returns to his work as a news reporter. After just three days on the job, he quits in order to prepare himself for preaching and leaves home the next day to attend Gordon College in Boston.

June 1948, June 1951: graduates from Gordon College, then from Gordon Seminary (Wenham, Mass.).

summers in the late 1940s: Harold is part of a three-man preaching team that itinerates throughout rural areas in northern New England and the Canadian Maritimes.

September 7, 1950: marries Jane Finch, from Everett, Mass., a fellow student at Gordon College whom he met on a gospel team. They continue to travel in a preaching/music ministry.

summer 1951: begins leading Sunday services for a Bible study group in Nashua, N.H., which on November 5 that fall holds its first meeting as the Trinity Baptist Church.

1951-58: Harold pastors the newly founded Trinity Baptist Church; children Jonathan, Karen, and Rebekah are born to the Burchetts.

1958-67: pastors Dover Baptist Church, Dover, N.H., where Stephen is born to the Burchetts.

1967-80: pastors Quidnessett Baptist Church, North Kingstown, R.I.

1979: Moody Press publishes Harold's first book: *People Helping People: How Every Christian Can Counsel*. Five other books follow.

December 1979: finishes Doctor of Ministry degree from Trinity Evangelical Divinity School, Deerfield, Ill.

1980-84: teaches full-time in the pastoral training program at the Graduate School, Columbia (S.C.) Bible College. Both before and after this assignment, Harold served for more than twenty years as adjunct professor at Columbia, teaching courses on biblical counseling and church life.

1984-91: pastors High Park Baptist Church, Toronto.

July 15, 1991: Jane has her first episode indicating early onset of Alzheimer's

1991-98: pastors Virginia Beach Community Chapel, Virginia Beach, Va.

1998-2010: Harold cares for Jane full-time at their home in Virginia Beach.

April 13, 2010: Harold and Jane fly from Va. to R.I. via Wings of Mercy; they enter a retirement and care facility.

August 22, 2010: Jane Burchett dies, sixteen days short of her and Harold's sixtieth wedding anniversary.

spring 2011: Harold joins New Covenant Christian Fellowship, Attleboro, Mass., where he later serves as interim preacher.

October 10, 2011: marries Cheryl Gale Johnson, longtime member of Quidnessett Baptist Church.

Part 1

God's Work in Me—First

Chapter 1

Childhood Conversion and Early Stirrings

My very earliest childhood memories are filled with a sobering reality of God at work, intruding and altering the way I thought and acted. This was simply the way I grew up thinking life was supposed to be.

Like any child, I did things I knew to be wrong. Early on, though, I was set against that behavior and wanted the Lord Jesus to rule my whole life. I was faced with two dilemmas: How could I be sure of life in heaven with the Lord? and How could I stop sinning?

This way of thinking for a youngster seemed very normal to me, given my upbringing. I was immersed in the church and was taught about God in my home by both parents and by all my grandparents.

My two grandfathers, both skilled carpenters, had with their own hands built a church building just around the corner from my childhood home. Organizing their friends and fellow carpenters, and with teams of ladies standing by to feed them, they amazed the community by erecting the entire structure, foundation to roof, in one day. All that remained was inside work. In this building I heard the Gospel from fiery evangelists who made sure that all of us who listened could not both sleep peacefully and fail to settle accounts with God.

One particular sermon, on the final judgment, is still vivid in my memory. Midway into the message, an electrical thunderstorm arose, and the lights suddenly went out. Taking advantage of the crashing thunder and the flashes of lightening, the evangelist cried out, "There! What if this were the Lord's appearing? Where would you be?" It seemed to this shaken child that the preacher was pointing directly at me!

I often sat there among the crowds that flocked to the adjacent outdoor tabernacle with its crude benches and sawdust-covered ground leading to the "mourner's bench" at the front, where I saw many a penitent begin a new life. Though I never found the courage to walk to the bench, I did search for God over and over again, praying down in our garden. Indeed, often while the jarring messages were going forth from the tabernacle platform, I was down in our nearby cornfield listening. There between the rows of ceiling-high field corn, I knelt in repentance and begged God to enter my needy heart.

My inner struggles did not soon end, however. Mom once discovered her younger son sitting up in bed and not sleeping. "What's wrong, Boy?" she asked in deepest concern. With heavy sobs, it tumbled out, "I'm not a good boy!" But how I longed to be! She immediately summoned Dad, and the two of them knelt beside me, one on either side, and we prayed together that I might be graciously received and forgiven. That scene some eighty years past is still a precious one to me.

And so it was that, early on, I learned the crucial lesson of basing my eternal assurance on what my Lord Jesus Christ did for me in my behalf when he lived here on earth, and not on what he had accomplished in my young life. After years of warring against doubts, I came to rest in John 1:12: "To all who received him, to those who believed in his name, he gave the right to become children of God." This is what the Lord himself promises, I reasoned, and he is the Judge. I shall forever rest the matter on his word. If necessary, I will recite that verse as my defense in the hour of judgment! A final prayer at my bedside concluded my uncertainty as to personal salvation.

My dad played a key role in helping me find my way spiritually. He knew how young children thought. Once during our evening Bible time, with my older brother, younger sister, and me circled in front of him, I asked him, "Dad, what's it like to be a real Christian?" I have never forgotten his classic answer: "Harold, it's better than eating ice cream!" Bull's-eye, for sure!

Thus it was, in my earliest memory, that God's Spirit impressed on me that I was to be his in a singular manner. Each phase of this book seems like a double-edged instrument cutting both ways. Not only was I doing things for God, but he was working in my life significantly. Layer after layer of my apparent strengths were peeled back by Providence.

My first recollection of an attempt to use Scripture in church was when I was eight or nine. The Sunday School superintendent asked a group of adults and youth for a favorite verse. I still remember my selection—Psalm 12:1—as well as my wonderment at his strange reaction toward my verse. As others shared Psalm 23 and other familiar passages, I contributed, "Help, Lord, for the godly are no more; the faithful have vanished from among men."

"Well . . . uh . . . thanks, Harold. Who else has a verse?"

I wondered then, and still do, why this verse is not a good one for us today. And if we're concerned about society now, I also see and feel the punch of this little psalm's final verse: "The wicked freely strut about when what is vile is honored among men" (v. 8).

Now, after more than eighty years of experiences with God's dealing, I am finally realizing something of what God is aiming at through the myriad of powerful spiritual episodes he sent my way. And I am thankful that he began early on.

Chapter 2

Jump Start into Adulthood

My move toward adult responsibilities began early. I was allowed to choose and take risks—and had to face the consequences. I delivered the local newspaper in all kinds of weather and occasionally had to deal with storms of ice, snow, and rain. The weather mattered not—customers expected their evening paper, and no mercy factored into the equation. Nor was my family's care a way of escape from foul weather, since we had no automobile. About this time I began to dream of raising chickens and soon added this to my busy mornings and evenings, along with football practice. The chicken business tied up all my few dollars and led to endless battles with weather, animals, disease, and the need to erect protective shelter. After storms passed through, I often would survey my losses in dead chicks scattered over the pens and had to figure out how to get on with my business.

At age fifteen I bought my first car and began driving. A compressed public school schedule allowed me to graduate from high school at age sixteen, and I took a job running a local food market. I had already put in a couple years of intensive Saturday work in a larger market, and I wanted to tackle this new job, where I had to figure out the meat counter as I went along. (I was the top man in our staff of three.) I'm afraid I was ill-equipped to handle our labor disputes. I once floored an ornery coworker with a single punch, and then, as ordered, he took the broom and swept the floor.

My employer proved to be anything but honest in his dealings with me, so in my very first summer at work there, I resigned. I was immediately able to start my next truly exciting adventure—as reporter on the local newspaper, the *Clarksville Chronicle*. They needed another writer at once, so they decided to try me, despite my youth and inexperience. They knew Dad, and that made the difference. I had one week to get myself ready for tryout day. First thing, I must learn to type! Somehow I got inside the closed high school building, went into the typing classroom, and copied the typing chart that showed all the correct fingering. Then I started practicing at home. Day and night for the next week, I worked at it, using all my fingers. By week's end, I could type well enough.

Wisely, the general manager, who hired me, and the editor sensed my shyness and pressed me to be more outgoing and intrusive. Immediately, I was into the swim of gaining admission into all kinds of events, interviewing people and writing up what I learned. Soon, the paper's top writer left to join our growing Second World War effort, and I became the lead reporter. All timidity had to be shoved aside, for every day was a high-powered adventure interviewing everyone from the jail turnkey to the governor. Daily I moved from the police station to the courtroom, to the scene of wrecks, murders, or whatever seemed like the news of that day. There was no way to do the job without getting involved deeply in the action and drama of each notable happening. It was great while it lasted, and it played a role in altering the way I looked at myself and life around me. But for all I saw of the world and its ways, they never held any great attraction for me. I still rather pity those who happily wear the "stylish" shackles of a worldly lifestyle.

Little did I realize that these exciting days would soon end. The military draft was drawing ever nearer, so I decided not to wait until called. Rather, I volunteered for World War II service in the Navy. I was now eighteen years old, having worked for the *Chronicle* ever since graduation from high school.

As soon as I resigned, the editor, general manager, and other staff persons stopped by my desk and expressed their congratulations that I had indeed stayed in such a rough-and-tumble "racket" as news reporting without joining in its way of living. "But," warned the editor, "you can't possibly live that way in the Navy!" I smiled and assured him that I planned on making no accommodation to what I knew to be wrong. "Maybe I'll come back a bit tougher—but no rougher!" (Several years later, on my return from duty in the South Pacific, I reminded the editor of this very conversation, making clear that credit belonged to God, who was still at work in my young life.)

Entering the Navy as a teenager and being assigned duty on a destroyer brought a huge, permanent alteration in my life. At once I realized I must either stand up and be counted or be overwhelmed by all my shipmates' questions and, at times, even ridicule. So I devised my own secret battle plan. Taking a notebook, I entitled the first page, "Carrying the fight to them." Beneath, I entered a log of the men I talked with about the Lord Jesus. I put down the gist of each encounter, noting the Scripture used and what printed material I gave out.

Sadly, the question I heard most often was, "Burchett, how can you have any fun believing that way?" One day I launched a counterattack. Laughing at my detractor, I said, "OK, I'll tell you exactly what I did this past weekend, and then you tell me what you did. After church, the beautiful, young organist I met there invited me to go horseback riding on their ranch in the valley, and it was great! And you? You don't even need to tell me—I know about your fun. I've seen you return to the ship dead drunk and sick to your stomach after an evening with the prostitutes. Don't tell me about your 'fun'!"

Our tall torpedoman once taunted me, "You can't live that religious stuff in a war, Burchett. Science is all that counts now."

"We'll see," I responded. "If we get shot up and begin to sink, you call on science, and I'll call on God. We'll see then how real God is."

Dramatically enough, this very crisis came later on to this man. We got advance warning of things to come during our first mission, which was very nearly a suicide mission. Our ship was ordered to leave the entire invasion force and go close up along the Marshall Islands, then occupied by the Japanese. We exposed ourselves like this in an attempt to draw their fire, which would enable us to radio back to our invasion force, waiting twenty miles out, disclosing the locations of enemy gun emplacements. Miraculously, the Japanese chose not to fire on our ship, and we escaped.

Another chief antagonist of mine was a giant Scandinavian fellow who stood side by side with me in battle stations for this same operation. During the ensuing invasion of the Marshall Islands, we were firing nonstop for maybe thirty-six hours. Amid all the gun smoke and horrific roar and pounding recoil of our big guns, my shipmate was shouting to me his penitent apology for his boastful ridicule. "We respect you! Don't ever change!" he yelled through cupped hands.

But God was not finished making his point. After I was dramatically removed from our ship in a one-man transfer, our destroyer was shot up terribly, receiving multiple direct hits. I learned of this when I was back in Boston, where I crossed paths with a surviving shipmate. He described a heartbreaking scene. Our dead and wounded were scattered over the deck, and the hardest hit among them, he said, were the torpedomen!

These experiences, coupled with the repeated sight of lives being destroyed in our ceaseless battle engagements, became a driving force in my call to leave my peacetime job as a reporter. After I was discharged from the navy and had returned home, I went back to my old job at the *Chronicle*. After working there only three days, I turned to the editor and said, "I simply can't do this anymore. I must go and preach God's Word." I left the next day for Bible college and seminary.

Chapter 3

Learning How
Powerful Prayer Is

All useful Christians must be enrolled in the school of prayer. Therefore, looking back over those long, tearing months in the South Pacific, I see with gratitude that God was bringing me into a new relationship with him through prayer. The ceaseless struggle to witness to all my rowdy friends on board (where I never knew of another professing Christian or saw another Bible), coupled with each long night standing watch on the flying bridge, taught me much about prolonged prayer. Nights under the stars as the ship rose and plunged under the swells, God met with me in prayer. Sometimes it was anguished prayer. My teenager's world was blasting apart, but as I looked into the beautiful night skies of the South Pacific, God drew near and spoke in his language to my heart. At times, I was so transported that I wished to be nowhere else than there with him. At these times, the war and my homesickness became incidental.

A climatic moment in my entire South Pacific experience began one evening seated on the fantail of the ship reading with misty eyes a stack of sixty-five letters that I had just received from home. They had finally caught up to our ship after many weeks of no mail. With choking emotion there at anchor just off one of the Solomon Islands, I made three definite requests to Jesus Christ:

1. That I might somehow be spared to see my parents again. (I had not seen them since the bus whisked me away for boot camp.)

2. That I could be transferred some place where I might have instructions on how to preach God's Word in daily witness to other sailors and how to answer their ceaseless challenges. (Often as many as six or eight would gather at a time around me, plying me with questions and taunting, "How can you have any fun when you go into town?"—meaning sex and drinking mostly.)

3. That I might receive further technical training in caring for the complicated sonar equipment. (Often it would malfunction or break down in submarine-infested waters, and the responsibility weighed heavily on me to discover and fix the problems, which put my entire ship in jeopardy, as well as any vessels we might be screening from submarine attack.)

The very next morning after this crisis time in prayer, I remember consciously saying inwardly, "I believe this is the day of answer to all my prayer!" Humanly speaking, this was utterly unthinkable. As we all knew, our future offered exactly two options: our ship would be shot up and maybe sunk, or else we would serve out the war fighting in the South Pacific.

Here is what happened later that very day: I received a summons by loudspeaker to go directly to the sonar officer's stateroom. Though I frequently got such calls, this time my heart was pounding so hard that I paused a moment before knocking. The officer sat at his desk with a serious expression, and there before him was a letter. It seemed to me that I knew exactly the news it would contain—but it was utterly impossible! How could one man on a ship in the middle of the Pacific ever receive an order to be transported off that ship? And how could such an order ever be carried out?

As to the first "impossibility," a seaplane had landed in the water near our ship and signaled to us that they had an official order for the captain. Our small boat brought the letter, which ended up there on the sonar officer's desk. It was nothing less than an order for the transfer of one man back to Chicago for advanced training in radar and sonar. The captain had selected me to be that man, and I was ordered to pack immediately. All my shipmates lined the starboard deck to see me ferried off to the nearest island, from which I was to make my way back home as best I could. It turned out to be a harrowing experience, but God got me through it.

So it was that all three of my urgent requests were fully granted. I got home again to see my parents, and for months in Chicago I reveled in the fellowship and instruction at Moody Church, even as I was getting the best of advanced training in radar and sonar.

Perhaps there are two special reasons for thrilling experiences in prayer early in a Christian's life. First, God is merciful in his dealings with those who are beginners. Second, beginners are often simple in their faith; they simply believe God.

Chapter 4

Lasting Life Lessons

In hindsight now, I see that four convictions embedded themselves very early in the way I live and think, each of which was part of God's preparation for what was yet to come for me.

1. *I must bear witness to Jesus Christ.* Get your flag up first. It's easier that way, rather than struggling to witness on the stage others set for you.
2. *I can lead.* True humility does not necessarily make one only a follower.
3. *I must reproduce myself by training others to do whatever I am doing.* By the time I was transferred from my ship, I had, on my own, trained one of the team of sonar operators to do all the maintenance work to which I was assigned.
4. *What I value most is deep intimacy with God.* Midnight fellowship during World War II with the God of the universe changed my life forever.

I believe there is some connection between these shaping experiences in childhood and youth and those I will relate. For example, I have often had quiet but very frank confrontations with those at the top in societal influence. From the beginning of my ministry I made it a point to talk to editors of the local newspapers. On one occasion, I looked up the city editor of a large, controlling publication—the main one in our whole state. I talked to him about the almost pornographic pictures appearing in the movie section of his newspaper. The burning question that made him stir in his chair was, "Please picture that section spread open in the lap and under the eyes of a child or young teen—or a man and woman, for that matter. What does it do to them?"

After the showing on TV of a demonic film addressed to and involving teenagers, a young woman turned up in one of our hospitals after having attempted to kill her child as an offering to Satan. I felt the challenge, picked up the phone, and asked to speak to the manager of the area TV station. This is how I put it to him, quietly but very insistently: "You will be interested to know the power of your communication. A baby girl lies at death's door in our local hospital. She was an offering of a teenager doing just what your program suggested." There was a long and almost audible silence on the other end of the line. Then, "Well . . . perhaps we could get together and talk."

"That's what I would like," I responded.

He arranged for a dinner meeting for the two of us and also his program director. After dinner he invited us to come back to his office complex, and the three of us spent several hours together. The results were marked. The manager poured out an avalanche of his anger regarding world conditions, our nation's politics, and (of all things!) moral deterioration. The program director and I became friends. He was later of immense help to me when, on another occasion, I presented a challenge to a different public media.

Through the personal arrangement of the channel manager, I was invited to New York to talk with a national television company's vice-president in charge of standards. It was quite a scene—an unknown pastor of a little church in New England talking turkey with this imposing lady of power, along with the program director for the network. She was silhouetted against a backdrop of other skyscrapers and office buildings of the city.

"You have come to the right place with your concerns," she said. "Everything the network airs is prescreened in the offices you see down this corridor."

God helped me with a quiet composure and yet confident insistence. I sought to make them see that their portrayal of Christians who believe the Scripture and love their God was so often derogatory and negative. "That's why I am here. I wanted you to see the white of the eyes of one of those you are misrepresenting." Looking for a way to put them on the defensive, I asked if they could give me the distinction between two terms often used in the media, "evangelistic" and "evangelical." They were neither clear nor confident in their response. "Shouldn't you know how those terms are used by the very people you are writing about so critically?"

I then gave my scriptural views on the solid Gospel and the very underpinnings of our nation and its history. "You see, I'm not a wild fellow, frothing at the mouth, but I represent many thousand and millions in this country who simply believe what the great men of our founding history believed."

God so assisted me that it was a powerful meeting with definite results. The official encouraged me to go to the office of their nearest competitor, another national TV network, which I did that very afternoon. It was another powerful encounter!

I declined an offer from the vice-president of the first network headquarters to go to Hollywood and present my case there. I felt at peace in my heart that I had done what I should and could at that point.

I have always sensed a calling to confront influence makers personally and directly, rather than participate in other more time-consuming public efforts, even though I might support them. My methods, however, have not always been accepted peacefully. More than once, I have received threats on my life.

Chapter 5

God's Care of Our Personal Finances

Any picture of my family's life would be incomplete without disclosure of how our finances were cared for by direct help of God. From my earliest childhood, I was taught to give a tenth of my allowance, which was one dime a week. Sometimes I would simply give the whole dime to the church offering. My lifelong standard has been: the tithe is the Lord's, then beyond that, I sought to give freely as I saw needs.

When I purchased my own car at age fifteen, I also began to share a little rent money with my parents. I felt boyhood pride in being able to do that. I have always lived by the principle of putting God first in finances and of staying debt-free.

An early test came when I received a reminder from my seminary's finance office that, in order to be graduated, all of my bills had to be cared for. This reminder was a severe jolt and drove my wife and me to earnest prayer, for there was no apparent way to squeeze any extra money out of our very limited budget. Sometimes we had no food left in the refrigerator and barely enough money for gas to drive to and from graduate school, where I was completing my last year of studies. I owed more than $200, a very sizable amount.

We experienced God's tender care as extra money came unexpectedly to us. One example I remember was a warm letter with a check from an out-of-state lady I had never met. She reminded me that I had once helped her son when he was traveling through our town on his way to a new job. He somehow found his way to our church, and we realized his need and kept him in our home for a week. His Mom's thank offering arrived in the nick of time, and I graduated debt-free.

Some years later I was guest speaker at a summer Bible conference. My wife and four young children were with me. There was a deep spiritual stirring and heavy conviction of personal sin among the people, causing anxiety to the conference director, who felt responsible to provide a lighter vacation experience for the people. My heart was heavily burdened for this assignment, and I spent much time praying out in the woods near our cabin. Then a heavy stroke fell. The director came by and, with obvious embarrassment, notified me that I owed the conference twenty dollars (a very large sum for me in those days!) for having brought a child or two over their limit for speakers. I simply nodded and indicated that I would come by the office before leaving the next day. Back to the woods I went to kneel in prayer. I was humiliated! I had no extra money and realized that any remuneration from the conference would be mailed to me later. I owed them right now! Another heavy factor at this time was my wife, who had taken a train back to Boston for hospital treatment of a serious, life-threatening ailment. We both felt she would be OK until I could come later with the children, but it turned out that her experience at the hospital was overwhelming for her, and she phoned me in tears. All this was a part of my burden along with the children, now under my care, and I tried frantically to quiet them and to prepare my next message.

On that final morning I went to my place of prayer and reminded God of my need of twenty dollars, wondering how he would help me out here in the pine grove. Next I went to breakfast with my children. We were interrupted by an apologetic man who dropped to one knee near my chair and said to me privately, "I hope you won't be embarrassed, but hearing of your wife's trip to the hospital made me wonder whether you might have a financial need. Would you please accept this ten dollars?" I thanked him sincerely, informing him that there was such a need and that this was an answer to prayer. After breakfast I hastened to my prayer place and thanked God, but I pleaded for the remaining ten dollars so I could leave without shame and embarrassment.

The tabernacle bell called me to gather my children and go deliver my final message. Our car was all packed, and we were ready to go to the office and settle accounts—except that I still lacked ten dollars. After the message, I was ready to go out the side door, across the small field to our cabin, where our car stood waiting. A line of appreciative people stood between me and the door, offering encouragement and promising prayer. One elderly woman I did not know took my hand and spoke very earnestly to me, and then she pressed something folded into my hand. I thanked her and put it in my pocket without looking at it. Arriving back at our cabin, I retreated to my place of prayer. Kneeling under the trees, I said, "Lord, ten dollars from twenty leaves ten; let it be." And it was—a ten-dollar bill! I gave my older son the two bills and asked him to run them over to the office. We picked him up on our way out and drove off debt-free.

A larger test was now about to come. I hastened to the big-city hospital, where my wife was to be released and restored to our home. This was my first experience ever with such an institution, and I knew nothing of their procedures. What a jolt then, when I was told that, before my wife could be discharged, I must go to the business office and settle the financial matters. I had naively expected that this would come later. The chief financial officer blasted me as soon as I entered, "Why didn't you respond to the finance statement I sent you?"

"What statement?" I asked. Then he inveighed against me, accusing me of irresponsible deceit. The thought suddenly came to me: Jesus Christ is Lord of the universe and my personal Lord; I am his, and this is his matter. So I walked straight to his desk, put both hands on the front side of the desk, leaned down toward him, and said, "I knew nothing about this regulation. I received no statement from you, and I will accept no abuse from you!" (I found out later that the statement had been sent to the wrong address.) He was stunned and began to stammer, asking how much time I needed to pay. I told him, "I don't have all that money in my pocket right now, but I will pay you in full, within thirty days."

He meekly replied, "That will be fine." And I left, taking my wife with me.

God supplied all the money needed within the prescribed time, and I mailed it along with the misaddressed envelope and statement. I was still debt-free!

I opted out of Social Security back in the 1950s, when the choice was allowed to pastors. When Medicare was later introduced and linked to Social Security, I was left without either. Furthermore, the churches that I pastored did not offer retirement plans. This way I chose meant living without savings and instead emphasizing giving. I should add that I have not preached that other people should follow this particular plan; it is simply the way I feel God led me.

At least it was the way he led me until the day my wife asked me solemnly, "You have the faith to live this way, and God has surely helped us. But what if you die and I am left with nothing and don't sense that same faith? Who will believe with me and for me then?" Deep in my heart I felt an instant agreement with her. Our children were now grown, and we needed to make decisions about a new segment of our lives and ministry. As I began to set money aside, I saw God work just as wonderfully as he had in caring for us for all the years without any bank account.

Chapter 6

Deepest of All the Trials

My deepest chastening and stretching experience, far worse than my years in World War II, was the nearly twenty years of caring for my wife, Jane, while she suffered with Alzheimer's Disease. Each new phase of the disease seemed more overwhelming than the one before.

I was pierced by the realization of what she herself was suffering, especially when I heard her cry out, "I'm ruining your life!" or "You, too? Are you also turning against me?" (spoken when I was attempting to correct her), or "I can't do anything right!" (when I discovered her weeping and asked why).

Once I found Jane seated at the piano in tears. She wanted so much to play, but her broken mind would not allow it.

My longing for at least some recognition or loving response from Jane invariably ended in further wounding. Sometimes I would kneel at her bedside and plead, "Please, Honey, look at me—just look!" No response, or maybe a look in the other direction. I might put her arm around my neck and ask, "Please give me a hug." Then her arm would slip off and flop to the bed. Such happenings taught me the great lesson that my love was not dependent on her response; it could exist without being "attracted."

Every caregiver for an Alzheimer's patient had best learn quickly not to look for brighter days—ever. This disease can only worsen, until death. A wonderfully valuable lesson I learned was to avoid all side glances at things I would like to fit into my schedule. Instead, I must simply run the race assigned to me by God, as the Bible teaches: "Let us throw off everything that hinders and the sin that so easily entangles, and let us run with perseverance the race marked out for us" (Heb. 12:1).

Always, as Jane's primary caregiver, I was in deep water, well over my head. I took solace, though, in Peter's experience on the Sea of Galilee. One day, while in the middle of the conflict, I wrote the following words:

> When Peter walked on water toward Jesus, it did not matter how deep the water was, so long as he was above it. Even when he was sinking, there was no danger because he had the good sense to call out to Jesus. I am well practiced in making Peter's desperate plea, "Lord, save me!" (Matthew 14:30). Alzheimer's waves are too much for any person. Good swimmers struggle more; I'm learning to call and rest. The Lord Jesus is bringing me into his new world, where swimmers sink and sinkers float. (*Last Light: Staying True through the Darkness of Alzheimer's* [NavPress, 2002], 136)

After nearly twenty years on this assignment, I was often so depleted at night that, after getting Jane on the bedside commode, I would hold one hand on her and rest on her bed, having the strength only to cry out to God for help in making the final cleaning and then in lifting her into her hospital bed.

Finally, crashing in all my systems, I called on Angel Flight, which lifted us into the arms of family in Rhode Island. I simply locked the door of our Virginia home and walked away. It was all I could do. My kids picked up the pieces, moving my stuff, and a friend and real estate agent in Virginia sold the home. We moved into a retirement manor—Jane in the intensive, twenty-four-hour hospice care, and I in the independent living section. At least we were still under the same roof, and I could be with her as much as I wished. Every night she slept on my shoulder, just as she had at home, while we watched *Wheel of Fortune* or *Jeopardy* in the Activity Room. After four months, she died peacefully in her sleep, as we had prayed.

On that last day, when I got the early morning knock on my door, I rushed to Jane's bedside and committed her to the Lord. Then, standing outside her door, I said aloud to all the staff persons mingling about the nearby nursing station, "The devil just took his best shot, and he lost! My Jane is with Jesus in heaven—death and the grave lost again!"

Now, at this writing, I am gradually emerging from the past twenty years out of circulation and am returning to life outside. This entire two-decade period I now consider to be the most valuable segment of my entire life. In a way, surviving each new day of each week, month, and year seemed quite like a new miracle. Repeatedly, and relentlessly, I was driven to cry out to God, "I can't function any longer; I'm completely broken down. If I am to take another step, you will have to make it possible." And somehow he did, day after day!

A moving scene comes to mind from a Good Friday several years ago. I was returning home with Jane from a calamitous attempt at a meal in a fast food restaurant. The event included Jane's boisterous outburst at the counter, followed by a spilled drink and a crushed sandwich at the table. Finally I escaped out the door with her and headed home to meet two women who were taking her for a hair appointment. Against her protests, I managed to get her into their car and sought to quiet her by reminding her again of Jesus' death on the cross, which we were remembering on this day. Nothing seemed to register. Asking the ladies to be patient with her, especially today, I waved good-bye and turned toward our front door. Tears began to rise as I entered the empty home. The radio was on, playing a beautiful rendition of "There Is a Fountain Filled with Blood." The floodgates opened, and I wept and wept.

Sitting down in my living room chair, I noticed that the very next song was one that Jane and I sang at our wedding, "I'd Rather Have Jesus." A phrase of Scripture again came to mind, "the fellowship of his suffering." I knelt by my chair and pictured myself on my knees before the cross of Christ. The doorbell rang. It was the lady who volunteered to help weekly with our shopping, who had arrived with groceries. Seeing my tears, she asked what was wrong.

"It's just hard . . . ten years ago this summer was the first episode." I quickly assured her that deep down I was happy in Christ. "Also, do you realize that I live with a wife who never sins? I would not change anything. God has finally released me from the burden of trying to be someone important."

Little did I realize then that I was only halfway through my test as primary caregiver for Jane. Ten years had passed—but there were ten tougher years ahead.

Now, dear reader, I will share what I did when the hurt grew impossible to bear. In my desperation, I would pray, "Lord, would you please hold my hand?" (His are warm, and those scars are still there! His body is really human; he was born there in Bethlehem. The spikes pierced those very hands that touched so many. Power is there today.) "Lord, fifty years ago you gave Jane to me to have and to hold till death parts us. Now she is being taken from me bit by bit. May I lean on you a little? O Lord, I hurt so bad!" I remember that once, right after such a prayer, the radio starting playing "What a Friend We Have in Jesus"—well-timed indeed!

This is simply my testimony of a life forced to focus on the Lord. Friend, do you think often of a new car? Try hugging that! Try holding hands with stocks and bonds! As the song puts it, "Take the world, but give me Jesus."

Have you perhaps lost confidence in the Christian faith, maybe being withered by the ridicule of a teacher or a friend asking, "Where is God? Let's see your proof!" Here is my personal answer: "This poor man called, and the Lord heard him; he saved him out of all his troubles" (Ps. 34:6).

On one occasion I wrote out the following important lessons I learned from all these years, along with the verses the Spirit used to rescue me:

1. How to keep going when you can't

    Those who suffer according to God's will should commit themselves to their faithful Creator and continue to do good. (1 Peter 4:19)

    My suffering fits this requirement, and the two suggested steps are mine to take; namely, commit myself to God and keep on doing good, putting one foot in front of the other.

2. How to overcome evil with good

    Do not be overcome by evil, but overcome evil with good. (Rom. 12:21)

    During the worst of Jane's angry phase, when she lashes out at me with physical and verbal abuse, I grasp her wrists to quiet her and look into her face and simply profess my love to her. "You have been such a good wife and mother, Jane, all these years. Thank you, and I love you." In time, God's Word proved so true. Alzheimer's does not know what to do with God's love.

3. How to love when there is no attraction

God has poured out his love into our hearts by the Holy Spirit, whom he has given us. (Rom. 5:5)

I find it absolutely impossible to love continually one who is utterly mangled in their person by Alzheimer's. Therefore, I am forced to God's fountain in order to supply what I do not have. He has poured his love into me, and I am able give it forth freely to Jane—but I must stay close by the fountain.

Part 2

God's Work in My Public Ministry

Chapter 7

Going Public

The very first experience I had in "public" ministry left me with a lifelong impact. I was asked to teach a small Sunday School class of young boys when I was about 12 years old. We met behind the piano in the main Sunday School room. After only a few weeks on the job, shocking news came: one of my boys had died in an accident. I anxiously reviewed my recent teaching, asking myself, "Did I make the way of salvation clear to little John Henry?" This death was one of the many, many such incidents that occurred in my ministry over the next decades.

All during my college and seminary training I was busy doing itinerant evangelism or opening closed churches as a short-term pastor. Being both young (in my early twenties) and inexperienced, I was much cast on prayer as my one hope. One of my first summers took me to New Brunswick, Canada, to a tiny town of farms scattered along a highway. There was no electricity or running water, and not even a village center. I arrived at an isolated old farmhouse where a Mrs. Grant lived, a widow whom everyone called Granny. Her singular zeal kept the little church open. In the dead of winter, Granny would snowshoe the two miles to the church, open it, and build a fire to heat the building. There was no resident pastor, and I had been invited to come and hold services for a week.

Thus it was Granny who welcomed me when I arrived that evening. The lamp flickered on the oilcloth-covered kitchen table, and she spoke almost prophetically to me. "Harold, I believe God has sent you here." Then she explained with deep emotion how all the youngsters she had taught in Sunday School (which she had kept open, since there was no pastor) had grown up and left during World War II. Now they were back home, but they no longer attended the church.

Then she said to me, "Let's kneel before God and ask that he stir them to come to your meetings and be saved." Her prayer thrilled my spirit as she solemnly prayed, "My heavenly Father, all these years you have cared for me, supplying me with wood for the stoves and food when my cupboard was bare. Now I know you will hear this prayer for my boys." Then she named them one by one. She encouraged me to preach with confidence because the Spirit of God was in this effort.

As our meetings began the next night in the tiny church, which seated fifty or sixty people, I boldly called on men and women to come to the front of the church and indicate their repentance and desire for salvation. All present were unaccustomed to such a move as this, but they started coming. The first one down the aisle was a new resident, a lady from abroad who had previously expressed her dislike for Granny. This once-imposing figure, now melted in penitence, was also the object of Granny's prayers. Next down the aisle came a man. When he gave me his name, I realized he was one of the very ones that Granny had mentioned in her prayer the night before. Two or three other strong farmers—all Granny's boys—also came forward.

Before the week was finished, most of the men on her list had made public surrender to Christ. On more than one occasion, when we were singing a hymn of invitation at the end of a service,

I witnessed Granny slip to the side of a man who was holding back. She would look into his face, put her hand on his shoulder, and he would melt and come to the front.

One notable exception (whom I'll call Wilson) held out, gripping the pew in front of him and almost shaking. But God was not yet done with him!

The following day I moved on to the next town for another brief series of meetings. To this day, I remember the heavy pressure on me and the feeling that I was completely washed out and almost unable to continue directing the meeting and bringing the message. Suddenly, a flatbed truck arrived just outside the church door. Piled in the back were the men from Granny's church. Seated in the middle of them was Granny herself, beaming with joy. Our little congregation lit up when all these farmers marched down the aisle, leading Granny to a place of honor among them. What singing we had! I was stunned beyond words to see Wilson, the recalcitrant one, singing loudest of all, with a radiant smile. As soon as the meeting was over, I rushed to him and gasped, "Wilson, what has happened to you?"

"Let me tell you!" he exclaimed. "When the meetings closed Friday night, I was troubled trying to sleep and fell into a dream. I saw all the people of the church marching through a great door to receive God's heavenly blessings, so I jumped in the line and marched with them. But when I arrived at the door, it slammed shut in my face, and I heard a great voice say, 'Wilson, you shall not enter!'

"At that I awoke in a cold sweat of fear. I rolled out of bed onto my knees and began to plead with God to save me also. And he heard me! One of our men is a chaplain with the Army. He happened to be home that very weekend and lined up all the newly converted men to have a great baptism. I went immediately to him and begged to be included. Brother Harold, I have believed and been baptized!" We both wept. Thus Granny Grant had all her prayers answered, just as she had asked.

Right after this experience, the man in whose home I was staying came to me following the service telling me he wanted to receive Christ and be saved. His wife was a leading lady in the church, and he was held in highest regard by all the townspeople because he was the government inspector of potatoes, the main crop in the area. But he was undoubtedly the most introverted, shy person of public responsibility that I have ever met. In his home he would barely speak, and it was always difficult to hear what he said. I was very surprised that he presented himself in this way as the congregation was leaving the church.

After briefly instructing him, the two of us knelt, and he began to pray a most remarkable prayer, with no embarrassment or hesitancy whatever. It seemed as if I was witnessing a wondrous conversation between this man and God, something like, "Thank you, God, for giving your Son, Jesus. Lord, you were right at home with plain people and talked so simply that all could understand." His prayer also carried him into the heavenlies, and as he described what he was seeing with the eyes of his spirit, I literally began to shake. He prayed eloquently for twenty or thirty minutes nonstop. In the middle of his prayer, while worshiping our Lord Jesus for his simple dealings with ordinary people, he interjected prayer for me that I might always keep my messages plain and understandable. Then he paused and said directly to me, "Did you get my message, Brother Harold?"

"Yes!" I replied, still shaking. He rose from that encounter a new man, and he and his wife raised both their sons to serve God.

Another summer I was invited to take a circuit of four or five closed churches in Nova Scotia, keeping them open at least for the summer. The pastor of the large in-town church that sponsored the ministry to the surrounding rural churches also lined me up to help in a summer youth camp for boys. There I became an instant celebrity because I could play baseball in the way they all wished to. They apparently were closely following American sports and especially admired American athletes. But it was quite a wild experience to be living among them. They were out of control, and the pastors who led the camp seemed unable to restore order.

I once saw one of the senior ministers with his hands upraised, crying out for a spirit of reverence and beseeching divine favor on his attempt to teach them, even as they were laughing and punching each other in disarray. Nor was this the worst of it. The youngsters were stealing the pastors' flashlights and personal belongings and refusing to go to bed when ordered.

In the mind of the pastors, I was simply an unordained helper. My heart, though, burned within me at the sight of such disrespect from the kids and lack of authority and strength from the pastors. Finally, in desperation, the pastors asked me if I would lead the next fireside meeting. I agreed, with one condition: "Let me handle the young people my way." I must remind the reader that I had not long been out of the Navy and away from the war and knew little about "proper" ways to handle such problems.

So now it was my turn to face the wriggling bunch seated on logs around the campfire. Some of the boys were already crawling away through the grass down the hill. With fists doubled and in a loud voice, I ordered them to put their backside on the log, and "The next one who moves, I'll pop you!" Apparently they believed me and stayed quiet, and I told them the Gospel in simple, direct words.

Walking back to our cabins, the pastors explained to me why the kids were so quiet when I was speaking: "It's because you're young, and they like that." I insisted, rather, that it was the message that held their attention.

The next night at campfire time it was raining, and the pastors realized that the meeting would have to be in the dining hall, where discipline would be even more impossible. So they asked me to speak again. This time the young people were quieter, and I simply told them, in story fashion, of Jesus coming to earth and dying on the cross. I described the punishment he endured and told them that it was because of the very sins that they were committing—the lying, stealing, and profanity. A hush came over them. I suggested that those who wanted to quit their sin and come to Christ should follow me out of the dining room, across the field to one of the cabins for prayer. With that, I simply turned and slowly walked out. My heart leaped with joy as I heard the marching of all the feet following me. In the dimly lit cabin the young fellows sat on all the bunks and filled all available space. Then they began to cry and pray and plead with God to forgive their sin. They were unsparing in their confessions. That night the entire camp was orderly and quiet.

I learned the following day that an older pastor's teenage son had gone by himself to the lakeside, weeping and begging Christ to forgive and cleanse him. That minister was the first of several to stop by my cabin the next day. It was clear that these pastors were humbled because they saw that the simple Gospel message, brought by an unordained and untrained younger man, produced results. Their conversations with me were all similar. They used to believe the simple way that I believed, but their graduate studies had put out their fire and turned them in a new direction. I did my best to admonish them.

These experiences involving pastors both perplexed and stirred me. On another occasion, I was asked to speak at a New England church whose pastor was about the age of my father. I was staying in his home. At the church, I gave a simple Gospel message, and in response, numbers turned to Christ. That night, he came to my room in his home and shared his heart with me, "I used to believe like you do, but somehow I've lost something." We knelt and prayed together.

I became convinced that all too many pastors were compromised and powerless, with many so weak that they were unable to lead and control even their own families. I started to think, "If this is what it's like, then I'll never marry." Later, after I had met Jane and before I ever proposed to her, I questioned her at great length as to her views on discipline and order in the home. Also in my conversations with her I brought up all the major doctrines, wanting to make sure we were of one mind. On one "date" I went through the entire book of 2 Corinthians, thinking that I needed to acquaint her with the way I thought a preacher's life ought to be lived and his home managed.

Resuming my story about my summer assignment among the churches in the Maritime Provinces, I recall a number of memorable experiences. The large city church that had oversight of the circuit of churches allotted to me was pastored by a man who sought to broaden my doctrinal views—especially on the atonement. I replied that I was settled in my faith that the blood of Jesus Christ was offered once for all for sin and that that was enough to satisfy God. I still recall the surprised look on his face as he sat in the packed church in one of my final Sunday evening services that season. Repeatedly, I had been told that people would not come out at night, either to the home Bible studies we scheduled most weekday nights, or to the church for Sunday evening services. But now here they were, packing every square inch of space! They sat on the pulpit stairs and in all the aisles, and even filled an adjoining room. In addition, people had been confessing their sin and turning to Christ even in the home meetings.

The very last meeting was held back at the largest church of my little circuit. It also was filled, and the meeting was very solemn. It became apparent that the entire congregation was under the conviction of sin and had a sincere desire to be made right with God. I tried first to have a public response and counsel each of the folks who came, but that was insufficient for the weight of conviction that was evident. The congregation stayed in their seats until I finished the personal counseling, and then, not knowing what else to do, I announced that all who wanted to truly be saved and confess Christ as their Lord should stand at their seats for a moment, then be seated. They did so, one after another, until it seemed that all, or nearly all, of the congregation had stood up. It was a very moving experience. I recall that one man who stood to his feet was a gentleman I had visited in his home. He laughingly said that he would not dare to come to the meetings because he had not attended church for some twenty-five years and felt sure that the place would fall in if he showed himself. But he came and was smitten in his heart by God's Spirit and stood in his turn. Later I dismissed the congregation and stood at the door to counsel and exhort them one by one. This lasted until about 10:00 P.M.

Incidentally, this church came alive and, on their own, decided to continue with a special series of evangelistic meetings. An invitation was sent to me in Boston to return and be the preacher. I was unable to leave my schooling at the time and had to decline, but the pastor back at the city church was so fired up in his heart that he offered himself to do it—and he did!

One last episode should be mentioned. The town sponsored a historical celebration and roped off the downtown area for the occasion. Gaming booths were installed everywhere, including on the lawn of the main church! I objected to the pastor, but he shrugged it off. Then I witnessed the spectacle of open drunkenness and lewdness (clearly against town laws), with the police just looking on and laughing. Little children were among those who lined the streets, laughing at those who cavorted in a so-called parade. My spirit burned within me, and I remonstrated at the church I was serving, announcing to them that I was asking God to send rain and wash out plans for the big night, which was yet to come in a couple days.

The evening of the main celebration arrived, and I went off to my regular home meeting nearby, still praying for a cloudburst. As soon as I was free, I returned to the city, where I witnessed that my prayers were abundantly answered—the heavens seemed to literally open up!

As I entered the city, I noticed that the band members for the big dance in front of the church were scattering in every direction. I saw only one remaining couple, clinging to each other, completely soaked in the downpour. Nothing remained of all of the booths and tinsel but soaked colored ribbons rushing down the drains. Parking my car, I ran through the square, laughing and praising God—and getting wet.

Apparently word got out about my prayer for rain, and some of the townspeople blamed me for it. I know this for a fact because when I later entered the dry cleaning shop, a customer and the clerk recognized me and expressed their respectful displeasure.

I did learn through all this that God truly was in partnership with me when I prayed properly. For example, on another occasion back in the States, I prayed definitely that God would interrupt the rain and allow us to have a much-needed service in a church that had no pastor. Also I was praying that somehow a noisy dance that was scheduled for next door to the church building would not interfere. Results were gratifying. The rain stopped, and the band never arrived, allowing some of those waiting for the big moment to come to our service next door. Thus I learned that God not only sends rain but stops it.

A piercing question put to me by a lady in 1948 while I was traveling around preaching in a tiny settlement in northern Maine still stirs my heart today. "When someone here dies, what do you suppose we do? There is no pastor. No one cares enough to open God's Word of hope. This is what we do: In the dead of winter we pile wood on a burial plot and keep it burning until it deep-thaws the ground. Then we bury the body. No pastor is there to say a word, no prayer, nothing—just our tears. Will you be like all the others and go back to the city and get all of your nice training? Even then, you won't be back to live with us, will you?"

I struggled to make some answer. Even though I made a choice to return to the safety and comfort of the school, this encounter added fuel to my burners!

My mind goes back to a picture I took of a small congregation in front of their white church in the same general area of Maine. They were without a pastor, and all the people excitedly posed on the special day of a service led by our three-man Gospel team. The photograph shows Joe, a young boy of about 12, in his scout uniform standing proudly in the front row. A sense of self-examination grips me whenever I look at this picture, for the very next summer I met Joe's father at his little store. Sadly, he told me the lad had died accidentally soon after our services.

Instantly, I thanked God in my heart that he had awakened me early the morning of that crucial service. While the two other team members slept, I headed off to the church alone to see if I could speak to those who might gather for Sunday School. I had no prepared message but took along the "Wordless Book." The superintendent happily gathered all the adults and children who were there, and I held up my little book and told them from the color pages the story of Jesus. As I remember, nine people openly responded to my evangelistic invitation. One of the first was little Joe. How glad I was, and am, that God prompted me to make that extra effort.

The final story is one I personally cherish, since it shows the great power of the Holy Spirit. I was asked to help for a week at a summer conference for children. They included Teddy, age 10 or 12, who was profoundly deaf and had never learned to speak. He was bright enough but was obviously frustrated by his handicap and would make strange vocal noises, disrupting the meetings. I recall inviting him to sit with me in my parked car, along with his brother on his other side. There we were, the three of us, with Teddy in the middle so I could draw him pictures and form words with my mouth. When I realized he could read a little bit, I opened the Bible to John 3:16, and we prayed for special understanding. This was to be Teddy's first close-up Bible teaching.

As we proceeded, his interest became more intense, and he showed marked excitement. At the top of my tablet I drew a stick figure and labeled it "God." Then, at the bottom of the page, I drew a figure with a hand upraised and wrote under it "Teddy." Pointing high up over our heads with one hand and way down below, I pointed to Teddy seated beside me and then to the figure at the bottom of the page.

After several attempts, I brought him to see that the bad in his life made the separation an awful one. This took perhaps a half hour of signing, grunting, mouthing words, printing a word or phrase on other pages, and appealing to his brother for his help in translating. Once I was sure of that point, I moved to the point of the Gospel and quickly drew a figure representing Jesus between God and Teddy. One hand of the Mediator was around God's outreached hand, and the other hand I showed gripping Teddy's hand. When he realized what this all meant, that Jesus saves him, he erupted in a profusion of gestures and excitement. Teddy pointed to his left hand and gripped it with his right and pointed up to God to show that he was joined to the Lord, and then he began to thump with his finger on Jesus in the middle and clasped his own heart.

But the remarkable work of the Holy Spirit was not yet done. As we prayed a prayer of gratitude, a thought came to my mind. Would it not be wonderful if this child, who had never spoken meaningful words in his life, could give his testimony before all the campers? I set about it immediately, prompting him. First, I printed in large letters the proposed testimony of three words: I LOVE JESUS. Next, I spent 15 or 20 minutes helping him begin to change his grunts and groans into a controlled sound. I would nod vigorously when his tones neared the right level. Finally, upon my nodded signal, he could say "Ah-ee." Near enough. Then all three of us celebrated the fact that Teddy was finally speaking.

Next we tackled "love." As I pronounced the "lo-," I would point at my tongue and then at his tongue. He rolled back his tongue and made a series of trial efforts at the sounds until we applauded him. Then we prayerfully tackled something like a "v" sound, which I signaled to be started by "uh." Another half hour or so was invested in getting him to pronounce "Jesus," which we all finally celebrated with more thanksgiving.

That night arrangements were made for Teddy to make his first public appearance as a speaking believer. All of the campers and staff sat in stunned silence as the director told them that Teddy wanted to give a public testimony of his new faith in Christ. At this point the camp's number one troublemaker stood on a chair, faced the group, and said in a loud voice, "Ah-ee wu-uv Yeeshus!" For a time, no one knew quite what to say. But everyone recognized that this three-word testimony was a message from heaven!

Chapter 8

My First Pastorate

My first settled pastorate was far from settled. Since Jane was expecting our first child shortly, I accepted a call to become the pastor of a Bible study group meeting on the second floor of a converted barn. On weekdays it was used as a day-care nursery. Our group numbered a couple dozen, counting children. Though there were plenty of large churches in the city, so far as I could determine from my encounter with the other ministers, I was the only one who held the basic doctrines of our faith. In fact, the city boasted of its reputation as "the graveyard of evangelism." I was warned, "Soul-saving meetings never work here!"

Jane and I shocked everyone with how little furniture we had when we arrived. We drove into town with her cedar chest in the back seat of the car, my desk strapped to the top, and the desk chair in the trunk. That was it! Also, we had no money except the several dollars in my wallet. Yet God helped us wonderfully.

I was interested to learn that a property right on South Main Street was available, so I approached the owner. He had just foreclosed on his previous renter and was reluctant to get involved with our poor group. He was a known figure in the city—an attorney and dealer in personal real estate. Upon hearing his reluctance, I looked him squarely in the eyes and said quietly, "Please think this over. If God wants us to have the property, I know it will be ours."

I still remember how almost mechanically he replied, "I don't see how I can be involved in this sale to you—but here's the key. I'll at least let you look the property over."

Before dark, our group was in the building. Together we praised God for the property we felt he was about to deliver to us. I remember one lady sitting on the winding stairs praying, "Lord, keep him awake nights until he agrees to sell this property to us." Soon he phoned our attorney and confessed, "One would think I had never sold property before—I can't get this one off my mind. I can't sleep. Tell them I'll sell."

Now came the next hurdle: we didn't have any money, not a dollar! So we all gathered in thanksgiving and yet earnest petition for financial help from God. Then we all were amazed at how the money came in. It had to be a miracle, because as soon as the banks learned that it was an investment to begin a new church, they refused to lend money to any of our members, even though some were long-standing customers. On behalf of our newly formed church, I approached a bank that had a board member who belonged to our little band. The head of the bank, ignoring his own board member, launched into an attack on me.

"We don't need another church in our city! Who are you anyhow? What cult is this? Where will you be in two years? Probably dissolved." I left him and went around the corner to a very notable attorney. We needed someone to represent us.

He was very gracious and listened attentively to my vision for a new church that would capture the interest of young people as well as adults. In a deep, powerful voice he said, "Young man, you've got something there, and I'm going to be with you all the way." And he was—he never charged us a penny!

I should add here that, within the two years that banker mentioned, he himself had died, and our church had tripled in size. As for the attorney, within the next two years, he was elevated to the state Supreme Court. Twenty-five years later, on the occasion of the church's silver anniversary, he wrote me a touching letter of remembrance.

All our members agreed that they should each make a public response at a Sunday service indicating they had truly repented of sin and believed in Jesus Christ as Lord and Savior. Week by week as they felt ready, they did so. I took each one aside and counseled them for an hour or two. I wanted to make very sure that their years of exposure to very liberal teaching did not now hinder their faith and understanding. These original members were quickly joined by dozens of others from all kinds of backgrounds. Our beginning group had only seven or eight teens, but every one of them eventually became involved in some form of Christian service.

A funny thing occurred one day when I was sitting behind the church building studying at a folding table. I saw a strange sight approaching me through the trees from a nearby home. It was none other than little Richard with his toy cap pistol drawn. In front of him, with hands raised in complete surrender, two of his buddies were marching solemnly toward me. They stood at my table as Richard announced, "Pastor, these ol' boys don't know Jesus. Would you tell 'em how? OK, you guys, now listen and get saved!" You can be sure I took advantage of the opportunity! Not only was our little gunman converted, but his older brother, his mother, and I had encouraging encounters with his dad as I visited the home.

Because of the magnitude of the ingathering into our new assembly, it was a challenge to me not to be overpowered by so many things happening at once. The moving of God's Holy

Spirit was especially evident one Sunday morning. A number were ready to confess their new faith in Christ, but I knew God's work was even deeper than that, so I continued the meeting long overtime. Even then, people were still not done calling on God. Finally, however, out of deference to the perplexed ladies who were watching over our nursery children, I announced that we would all take a break and come back at 3:00 P.M. for a longer "evening" meeting. By midafternoon, everyone had returned, and it was a glorious time! After brief words from me, I simply asked that people stand and express their need, adding that I would then pray and counsel them right then and there. First up was a visiting university student. He wept as he explained he did not really know Jesus Christ as his Savior. That moment changed his life. With tears and praise interspersed, our service continued into the night.

The young man just mentioned was from a large church at the head of the square. His parents were shocked to hear of his visiting the "new church." They were even more shocked when he informed them that he wanted now to quit the university and go to a Christian graduate school. Within days the young man appeared at my door, along with his older brother. Seated in my study, the older brother attacked what he thought were our narrow views. I patiently answered him, though his arguments were not nearly as profound as he imagined. He was simply caught up in the notions that were most current in the day, mainly emphasizing love. No matter how I reasoned and pled with him, he simply became more defiant and abusive. As he left, taking his newly converted brother with him, I fell on my knees. I felt a heavy choking in my throat and chest and cried to God in Christ's name for victory over Satan. The very atmosphere seemed spiritually charged and weighed heavily on me.

A few hours later the phone rang. It was the older brother. Very apologetically, he said, "I was the one talking about love, but you were the one who showed patience and love toward me. I would like for us to talk again." The next day when he arrived, I could see God was already deeply working in his life. The final outcome: both went to a Christian school, and the young man became a missionary. His older brother, after marrying one of our church's young women, became a pastor.

Chapter 9

New Lessons in Ministry

An urgent call came to me from the local hospital. A young child of perhaps ten years of age who had attended our church a couple of times with his widowed mother had been severely injured and was at the hospital. I found the mother in a side room in tears waiting for some word from the examining medical team. It was obviously a very serious injury. She pled with me, "Can you find out anything from the doctors?" I located the team working on him in a room down the hall. To my surprise, the doctor stood and welcomed me with obvious relief. Concluding that I was the boy's pastor, he told me abruptly that the child had just died and then urgently asked me to inform his mother. I agreed.

The walk down the hall was a hard one. I tried to rehearse just what I would say, but nothing seemed right or easy. I pled with God to help me, as this was a new experience. Opening the door, I was met with the mother's anxious, inquiring gaze, and I said simply, "He has just died." At that, she shrieked and fell back in her chair. A couple of nurses came running to attend to her with medicines. I stepped out of the room. I immediately heard the mother cry out, "No, no, I don't want that! Bring back that young man with the Bible." I decided early and once for all—be a man with the Bible! The last scene I remember about this family is the picture of kneeling in her home with her other son and each of them praying their first audible prayers, asking that Christ might save them.

Another tough challenge came in the same hospital when, on my way home from an evening appointment, I decided to make a late-night stop at the hospital to see how a young child of eight was doing. As I recall, a childhood disease has left her with swelling in her brain. What a sight met my eyes! By the dim lighting I could see the young girl seated in the bed, writhing and groaning and clutching at the air while the mother leaned over her, raining down tears. Recognizing me, she looked toward me and gasped, "Why?"

I knew this was no time for theological profundities, but at the same time I wanted her to know that no charges were due God. Sin was our universal problem, and Christ was her answer. Such experiences caused me to think ever more deeply.

Two other experiences with death embedded themselves in my heart and mind. A young man of twenty-seven, clasping his wife's hand, wept over her hospital bed as she slipped away into the embrace of death. Presently he stood up and asked, "Would you be willing to tell my kids of their mom's death if I bring them to your home?" I agreed, and that afternoon he was there with his little tribe of three young children. I held one, the young dad held another, and the oldest sat between us as I told them the sad news. Children often do better than parents, partly because they don't take it all in at once. How glad I was to turn this story to that of life in Christ Jesus! Here was solid help for the children, as well as for Dad.

A similar incident occurred in Toronto, when a young father of four children begged me to come at once to his home, where his wife lay dying. A firm believer in Christ, she died shortly after I arrived. The children had already gone to school, so I went there and asked the principal to release them to me. He kindly gathered them into his office, where I told them of their mom's death, which, by the way, had been impending for some weeks. After briefly assuring them of her eternal life in Christ, we prayed and left for home. Since the undertaker had not yet arrived, the little family of five, including Dad, gathered around the mother's bedside. It was a very precious time of the near presence of the resurrected Lord Jesus Christ.

A turn into a new way came the very first weeks of ministry in a church I pastored for more than nine years. The sanctuary had a very formal decor with a divided choir—men and women separated and singing toward one another. A smaller reading desk was on the one side, and an elevated circular pulpit on the other side extended itself out toward the congregation. Indoor columns stood in a row down the two sections of the pews.

At first I declined their invitation to be considered as a prospective pastor. My way of public ministry might not fit there, I thought at first. Later, I willingly accepted their call. The first Sunday I preached brought a response to the public invitation of some seventeen people, mostly adults, but also some younger ones. The next Sunday eighteen more presented themselves publicly in repentance and confession of Christ.

Now how was I to care adequately for thirty-five new believers? This was a marked milestone in my entire life. I began making a series of progressive steps from forming a weekly new convert's class to the emergence of my own plan of individual discipling, which I called *Spiritual Life Studies*. The large essential decision came at once: I must multiply myself, training some, who then can train others. First, I prepared others to take charge of the new convert's class, which continued to meet. Later, as I began individual discipling sessions, a host of men and women were prepared not only to help new believers but also to further strengthen each member.

The judge made our evening service a memorable one. He was a faithful member in our church and a federal judge who had authority over a large number of other judges. People knew and respected him for his Christian witness. I once involved him in a dramatic Gospel presentation, emphasizing the propitiation of Christ's blood-offering.

To a filled church, I introduced my subject and then had the judge, in his judicial robes, stand at the pulpit and explain the place of all law. He said simply, "There is no answer to broken law unless the sentence be exacted. The guilty one might cry and cajole, but that will not change one thing. You might even bring your mother to plead your case and weep on your behalf. That will not change my decision. The law stands, and I must stand with it.

"Even if the criminal begins to threaten me, he can do nothing! The entire government of the United States is behind me. If necessary, irons will be clamped on the defendant, and he will still face the sentence and pay the price."

At this point I stood and explained propitiation, the one amazing sacrifice of Christ that satisfies divine justice in our stead. By Christ's suffering of death as our substitute, he answers to all the laws we have broken, and we are declared innocent.

None of those attending that service will ever forget this message and I was encouraged to stay by the cross in all my ministry.

Undoubtedly sent by God, special people have crossed my path at seemingly appointed times, from whom I learned valuable lessons. One of these was Mr. Norman. When I was in my second pastorate, Mr. Norman appeared one day at my office and asked to speak with me in private. "God showed me one day sitting in church by one of the sanctuary pillars that he would make me a pillar in this church. I'm not altogether sure what this means, but I wonder what you think of it?"

I was somewhat dubious, but yet somehow intensely interested in this fellow. Now an older man, he spoke with emotion about opportunity lost in his early life. Apparently he turned aside from God's call into Christian ministry and settled for a life doing odd jobs. His was a lonely life, having married a domineering wife who considered herself to be a minister and held services on her own in their home—much to his chagrin.

All along, however, he fostered his spiritual yearnings by years of intensive Scripture memory and by studying the writings of older saints such as Matthew Henry and Charles Spurgeon. He left me in awe by his ability to quote whole books of Scripture, even the long prophets. At once he set about to begin his new calling with us—or, I should say, with me—because it became increasingly evident that his life focus now was on upbuilding me and my ministry.

Deep in my heart I sometimes wondered if Mr. Norman was really of this earth! That peculiar shine in his face, his influence over servicemen in the church as they would gather on Saturday night for prayer with "Brother Norman"—and how he could pray! I sometimes peeked to see his kneeling figure as he with raised hands described, as it were, the scene in heaven with Jesus at the right hand of the Almighty. All of us were deeply stirred every week, and a number of these men keep in touch even to this day and mention "old brother Norman."

Most Saturday nights, even in a winter snow, he would show up at my door interrupting my final studies to pray briefly with me and then leave. Sometimes before he entered I was having difficulty getting my sermon thoughts together, but his "interruptions" invariably changed everything. Points of truth fairly jumped out of Scripture at me when I closed the door behind my brother. Not only the church but my family also was deeply affected by this man. We all loved having him with us for a meal.

News came to me one summer that he was taken ill on a trip into northern New England. I was able to drive over from our vacation spot to the hospital where he was. Those were to be his last days. He told me with deep emotion of a profound spiritual assault by Satan. Now in his great physical weakness, the enemy reminded him of the years he had spent out of God's first plan for his life. I was gripped by his very real description of the enemy's appearance. "And what did you do?" I asked.

Gathering his remaining strength, he said firmly, "I could only cry out, 'Grace! Grace! The grace of our Lord Jesus Christ.' With that, the devil was silenced and had to withdraw." I met his nurse, who was an unusually beautiful woman with a quiet composure. Very earnestly, she reassured me, "Don't worry about Mr. Norman; I will take care of him." I knew she was God's messenger to this aged saint, who had no one else on earth.

Chapter 10

Struggle of Life against Death

The phone call was urgent: death had just taken the only child of a young couple who were active in our church. Shockingly, the baby girl died right in the arms of the doctor, who thought he was making a routine checkup; the little one was not to be revived. The parents had long prayed to have this gift from God, and now she was gone!

Speeding to the home, I kept asking myself, "What will I say to them?" Prayer to the rescue! The familiar Proverbs 3:5–6 came to my mind and heart:

> Trust in the LORD with all your heart
>> and lean not on your own understanding;
> in all your ways acknowledge him,
>> and he will make your paths straight.

Here was the counsel God seemed to supply: "Bill and Joan, this is not the time to think and question things. Your burden is impossible for you to bear. Don't even think right now. Put it on the shelf [everyone needs a 'pantry' for such times] and leave it there until you are more sure of yourself. Visit the matter only with the Savior supporting you. Just as light always drives out dark, so God's power overcomes death." During the public visiting hours, the beautiful, tiny form lay in her small casket while the mother and dad stood with quiet smiles to greet everyone who entered.

I had a different experience with death when I visited an older man in his hospital room. Realizing that death was near at hand, he readily admitted his anxiety and fear, saying, "And there is nothing I can do to rescue my heart from this dread." He looked right at me for some help.

The Scripture I read him was 1 John 4:18: "There is no fear in love. But perfect love drives out fear, because fear has to do with punishment. The one who fears is not made perfect in love."

Confessing that he did not possess this peace and its root of love, he at once asked. "How do I get it?"

I read the next verse of the text: "We love because he first loved us." Presenting Christ and his loving sacrifice on the cross was easy to do at this point. Without hesitation, the man responded and died in peace and quiet composure.

Complete chaos greeted me when I rushed to a home not far from where I lived. It was just before dawn, but the house was alive with excited men and women, literally wringing their hands and rushing from room to room. I knew none of them except for the dying lady whom I had recently helped to know Jesus.

"Do something quick!" one lady cried in desperation. At this point I was standing quietly at the bedside, prayerfully surveying the situation. Her body jerked a few last times and then lay still, forever. I turned to the crying woman and the others and said quietly, "All that needs to be done has already been done—2,000 years ago." Then I presented the Gospel and informed them that this deceased friend and family member had received and believed this message. All of my hearers became still and listened.

Another emergency call pressed me to leave immediately after the Sunday evening service benediction to drive to the hospital, some twenty miles away, where a middle-aged man lay near death. When I arrived, he was still conscious, with his wife and two teenage children gathered around his bed. Just as I stepped into the scene, the doctor came to give the wife his assessment of the case. "Death is imminent," he said, "but I can stay it off by use of extraordinary means to stimulate his system and possibly even have him sit up again. However, he will surely regress and be subject to much more suffering and death. What is your choice for him?" With that, he excused himself from the room to allow me to counsel with her.

"Pastor, what do you think?"

"Let's pray," was my immediate response. As is so often in my experiences with God in prayer, a Scripture came to my mind, and so (thinking of Matt. 7:12) I faced the anxious woman with this question, "If you were the one there in bed and he stood here with me, what would you want me to say to him?"

Without hesitation she said, "I would want to be allowed to die in peace."

"Why not grant him the same release?" I asked.

She told the doctor her decision, which turned out to be a moot question for, when we arrived back at the bedside with the waiting children, the nurse was calling for the doctor to come at once. The patient expired right before our eyes.

This dramatic turn afforded a priceless opportunity to make eternal matters very real and have Christ stand with us there at the bed and receive the departing spirit of the loved one. As soon as the medical team withdrew, a complete peace settled over our little band. God was very near.

Helping children is ever a special challenge. I happened to discover a young boy of perhaps eight or ten seated against the far wall, grieving by himself in the funeral home's viewing room. Drawing a chair close to him, I asked quietly, "Is that your mom's body up front?" Still sobbing, he nodded yes.

With a quick silent prayer to heaven asking God's help, I proceeded in this way, "Are you bothered at the thought of your mother being buried in the ground?" Immediately he nodded that he was. "Do you know that your mother will not be put in the ground? Only the body-house she lived in. You see, I am not a body, but I live in this body. You're not just a body, but you have that one as your house on earth. Up front there in the casket is the house your mother lived in, but she herself is not there. Because she believed in Jesus, she is now with him where he lives—in heaven."

The lad ceased crying and received my words with understanding and apparent agreement.

Frequently when I arrive at a scene of impending death, I am left to figure out whether the person is really conscious and whether this is a final spiritual contact with them. An example of this question came once as I rushed to a nursing care facility. "He is completely unconscious and no longer responding," was the family's sad greeting as I arrived. I went to the bedside, saw that he was an older man, and wondered if he was a believer. It was with God's guidance that I burst into singing, "Rock of Ages, cleft for me, let me hide myself in thee." Almost immediately, I saw his lips begin to move, and he sang with me the rest of the hymn (much to the amazement of the family members)!

Mr. Munson's terrible accident brought me rushing to the local hospital. The farmer had been found out in the barn with an awful head injury, the cause of which was never determined. His skull was cracked across the back from ear to ear. I could not recognize him, even to tell if he was male or female. His whole face was swollen, and his eyes were tightly closed and bulging. The nurses intercepted me outside his door and warned me that he was a shocking sight, unconscious, would likely die very soon, and furthermore, if he lived, he would never regain his mental faculties. While they stood in the doorway, I approached his bed and called to him. "Mr. Munson, it's Pastor Burchett." With great satisfaction, I was sure I saw him give a very, very slight nod. Then I urged him, speaking close into his ear, "I know you are hurting. Let's pray. I will help you to call on God for yourself. You say the words right after me." And he did, with barely audible sound.

"Lord Jesus, I have sinned against you. Now I am in great need. Forgive my sin. I believe Jesus died for me and is now in heaven. Lord, come into my heart and save me. Amen."

I prayed briefly and turned toward the two or three nurses standing in surprised silence. "You see, this is why I don't quote nice poetry to dying people. They need and want God." With that, I left them to think their own thoughts.

Mr. Munson not only did not die, but he lived with all his faculties intact and returned to farming. I saw him many years later when I returned for a special service at the church where he had become a regular member. He sat beaming on the very front row with his family.

My phone brought an urgent message. A man was dying at the hospital, without any hope of salvation. I did not know the gentleman very well because he had resisted any of my previous efforts to talk with him.

Hurrying to his room, I found him lying on his side with his face toward the wall and obviously in a very weak condition. I moved around the bed in order to place myself in front of his half-opened eyes. At this, his eyes opened wide. He made not a sound, but with all his remaining strength managed to roll over in bed so as to turn his back to me. I was certain he recognized me. "What is the right thing to do under these conditions?" I asked myself. I was also certain that any further pleading not only would be ineffective but would cheapen the glorious Gospel. He had now finally confirmed his rejection.

Without another word, I walked directly from the room. In the hall I stopped, turned back toward his door, and fought the battle one last time. "This man is at the door of death, and I have brought him his final call. He will perish forever in hell, yet I cannot decide for him. He is responsible before God." In deep anguish but still decided, I turned again and left for my office, less than two miles away.

No sooner had I reached my office than the secretary said, "This call is for you." It was a hospital nurse informing me that the gentleman had just died.

Snatched from the jaws of hell! Even that is an under-statement of what happened to my friend's older brother. God had used me to bring my friend to Christ several years back, and now the focus was on his brother. Both were middle-aged men. The father of the two men had, for a while, lived with this older brother, who was definitely not a believer, nor was his wife. Because of the dad's attempted testimony to them, they threatened to put him out of the house if he spoke to them about Christ again. I also had little success in penetrating his barriers.

Things changed quickly. He became a sick man and was taken to a hospital in another city where he lapsed into unconsciousness before the eyes of his two anxious daughters. Before his brother raced to the hospital, he and I prayed that God might spare the older brother long enough to believe. It should be pointed out that the last time the subject of salvation came up in a telephone conversation between the two men, the older one abruptly hung up. Our fellowship of men had special prayer for this crisis situation, praying that God himself would guide our brother and commission him for this visit. On arriving at the hospital, my friend found the two daughters sitting beside his brother, who had lapsed into a coma with heavy breathing.

This, then, was the scene. While several of us prayed in my home, our friend found himself in the middle of this critical struggle between life and death, heaven and hell. One daughter directly informed my friend that, some hours ago, her sick dad had sat up in bed and clearly stated, "My brother is right—there is an awful place called hell!" He lay back down with an expression of utter terror on his face.

The daughter continued her report to her uncle. Only a short while later, her father's heavy breathing again stopped and he sat up and clearly announced, "I have chosen Christ as my Lord and Savior!" Again, he lay back down.

The dying man had one more pronouncement to make. He said clearly, "An angel now stands right there in the corner. He will soon take me to see my Father." With that, the dying, unchurched man began to sing *Amazing Grace*. Not knowing what to do, the doctors called for the hospital chaplain, who came and heard him singing. He commented, "Your dad must have been a truly religious man."

All this information greeted my friend when he arrived. Following my suggestions, he at once knelt beside his brother and, with his face close to the ear of the dying man, led in a prayer of thanksgiving for the wonderful news of his brother's entrance into the kingdom. "And I love you, Brother." All during this exchange in prayer, the heavy breathing quieted. But not long after, he died.

I conducted the funeral service, which was attended by a host of family and friends, including all his golfing buddies. I addressed them with complete frankness, saying confidently, "I am positively sure that our departed loved one and friend would want me to tell you, line by line, what he himself said just before he died." A holy quiet came over that audience, and I was able to talk freely to the attendees. My key scripture text was Hebrews 9:27-28:

> Just as man is destined to die once, and after that to face judgment, so Christ was sacrificed once to take away the sins of many people; and he will appear a second time, not to bear sin, but to bring salvation to those who are waiting for him.

The following account is so pertinent that I will retell it directly from *Bringing Christ Back*.[1] The reader will notice that the unusual evidences of God's power really were launched through the very ministries that churches ought always to be carrying out.

> Life was completely disrupted—or, I might say, smashed—for Ronald and Sarah, a handsome,

---

[1] Harold Ewing Burchett, *Bringing Christ Back* (Bringing Christ Back Ministries, 2006).

affluent couple in their prime years, just before an early retirement. Sarah was stricken with a rapidly progressing terminal cancer. Always the strong, energetic one, she was now emaciated and in such pain that she was barely able to move around in her house. When I visited the home, Sarah was realistic about what was ahead—days in bed relying on morphine to cope with the mounting pain, then death. She confided that the nights, with the excruciating pain, already were becoming a terror to them both.

Immediately, I perceived that reading Bible verses to her on the subject of comfort would be inadequate to sustain her through the long hours of struggle. I chose instead to employ a kind of discipleship counseling, hoping to bring a change that would continue within her permanently. She desperately needed equipping for her greatest-ever challenge.

It was apparent that Sarah had a personal faith in Jesus Christ, but her husband, Ronald, did not. A few questions quickly disclosed that her spiritual history had left her unprepared for what she faced. As I inwardly prayed for guidance, Sarah's need became obvious: she must gain a vital, more confident access to God in prayer to sustain her in the long hours of searing pain. Accordingly, on that first visit I determined to center everything on one issue: how does one truly pray in Jesus' name? I pressed her to put in plain words what that concept meant. "Just saying the words 'in Jesus' name, Amen' is not enough," I explained.

"After all these years of closing prayers with those words, I must admit that I do not understand what

I have been saying," was her frank admission. I was glad I had come, for here was one of God's children locked in a struggle with our last enemy, death, and very unprepared.

A new light came into her tired eyes as she realized in a fuller way the privilege of bringing her heavy load to the Father in heaven. Her faith mounted up as she clung to the new insight that her prayers—racked and rattled though they might be—were dear to the Father because they were presented in his Son's name, in his perfect merit. How she relished that truth, speaking of it (and practicing it) over and over again! "Now in the dark nights, I can stand before God and be heard!" she declared.

On my next visit there, I had in mind two objectives. My first one was to ask her, "Do you think of the Holy Spirit as a real person?" (I reasoned that she needed a very *personal* ministry of the Spirit.) After drawing out her thoughts, I discovered that regardless of what "doctrinal statement" she might personally have agreed to, she in fact did not conceive of the Spirit as a person.

Ignorance regarding the Holy Spirit seems to hamper or limit the Spirit's work within his children. To the extent that the ignorance is allowed to exist, something we might call a "willing ignorance" (see translations of 2 Peter 3:5 for this concept), the Spirit must surely be grieved. Regardless, my suffering friend was now eager to have the full assistance of God's Spirit and she earnestly asked forgiveness for her careless neglect of this gracious person.

Now, with the Spirit helping her, the previous week's accent on prayer became even more meaningful. A light was now shining in her dark night. But more needed to be done. My second objective for this visit was to talk to her husband about his own spiritual life. Outside, with Bible open on the trunk of his Mercedes, I urged him to repent of sin and trust altogether in the Lord Jesus.

"I can't do that," he objected. "I know so little about God or the Bible. In fact, this is my first conversation like this in my entire life." That very evening, however, he uttered his first audible prayer—childlike, but genuine.

It now became possible to institute the holy alignment prescribed in 1 Corinthians 11:3, where God, Christ, man, and woman are related in a proper way: "Now I want you to realize that the head of every man is Christ, and the head of the woman is man, and the head of Christ is God."

"Beginning this very evening, you must help your wife with Scripture."

"Wait a moment!" he interrupted. "I know nothing about the Bible, and she has been at this for years."

"I quite understand that, but you are her husband, and God will bless what you share. He will help you do it. First tell her what you have done here with me. Then begin reading together through the Gospel of Mark, a portion each night."

Beside these visits with Sarah, I saw that she had edifying visits from others in the church, and I scheduled weekly discipling with Ronald, using my Spiritual Life Studies. The results of this investment were marvelous indeed. During the distressful nights "we now have something definite and helpful to do," they told me with joy. With Ronald's gentle but enthusiastic leadership, they read through book after book of the Bible until the end came. And so it was that counseling with truth was infused into a suffering person's life, hour after hour, right from within the home. How could weekly professional appointments match this?

Honoring her request that I try to be present when her hour of death came, I went to the hospital where she had been taken one afternoon and decided to stay through the night. She was still lucid, but I sensed that the end was near. Shortly before dawn, I rose from the uncomfortable waiting-room chairs and went again to my friend's room. Sitting there with her were her son and daughter, one on each side holding her hands. Her husband, Ronald, was at that moment rushing back to her room. I soon indicated to them that she was about to leave us. Close to her ear I whispered encouragement, and as she was dying, I read these words: "The time has come for my departure. I have fought the good fight, I have finished the race, I have kept the faith. Now there is in store for me the crown of righteousness, which the Lord, the righteous Judge, will award to me on that day—and not only to me, but also to all who have longed for his appearing" (2 Tim. 4:6-8).

In a peaceful quiet, her body stilled. I then read the final words of the selected text again, applying them to Sarah's life and appealing to the son and daughter to place their faith in Christ. At that moment Ronald returned, and we all stood at the bedside for a final commitment.

Following the funeral, one thing remained. I continued weekly discipling sessions with Ronald. By the time the planned meetings were finished, he was functioning very well and continued on in his new faith.

I have related this account in some detail to show the strength and potential of our spiritual resources to help individuals in crisis. It is true that I, a pastor, took most of the initiatives here, but there were dozens of others in the church who could have done so, and some did share in this ministry. What I did was not because of professional position but simply because the need came to me and I chose to take it up myself. A properly equipped church has a company of men and women who know how to counsel, support, and disciple. In this story, notice how each of the three resources listed earlier came into play.

First, the wife and the husband were each, personally, cultivated spiritually. Next, they were moved forward in grace so that they might in turn minister to one another, and they were helped to reach out to their unreached children. Finally, my task also included the bringing of other ministering ones from our church fellowship into this home of need. (132-36)

A blaze of glory!—that's the only way to describe the departure of my good friend's sister. He introduced me to this very zealous lady, who had come home from an African mission field with cancer and was facing her impending death. My friend warned me, "Be prepared for a surprise when you meet her. She is both zealous and different. I predict that she will go out of this life in a blaze of glory. It is always that way with her."

Surprises from this missionary lady came thick and fast to me and our church. First, she married a fellow who was totally unable to see. Then, after her disease worsened to the point where she was bedfast and in great pain, she decided one Wednesday night to get up, dress, and drive to our prayer meeting. Looking haggard but determined, she asked if she could address the congregation of 100 or so people. None of us will ever forget her words. They went something like this: "I am dying, but I want you all to benefit from my experience. Permit me to tell you exactly what it feels like." Graphically, she unfolded her story and pled with everyone present to know the Savior and make full preparation for their own date with death. Later on, she was taken to a Boston hospital, and I heard reports of the impact she was making on nurses and doctors alike—so much so that the surgeon declined to perform any autopsy on her, and I noticed how the nurses spoke in awe of her.

I return now to her husband, who had lost his sight but who had keen hearing. As he sat by his new bride's bedside, only a few days before her death, his sensitive ears recognized a voice from his past. Making his way over toward the one he heard speaking, he asked the name of the visitor and was much elated to discover that this was the very man who had led him to Christ many years earlier, while he still had his eyesight. He told the man the story—how he was hitchhiking, how the man had picked him up, and how the man, in conversation in the car, had led him to faith in Christ.

Bursting into tears, the older Christian poured out his story. "Only today I told God of my complete discouragement because my testimony never seemed to bear fruit. I begged him this very morning to show me someone who has believed because of my testimony. You are the answer to my desperate prayer!"

Exactly as I had begun to expect the dear missionary lady exited this life in a blaze of glory that was the talk of her attending staff of doctors and nurses. They made an immediate decision that there should be no autopsy, out of honor to her.

Chapter 11

Getting beneath the Surface

Now for the first time I will relate a powerful encounter I had with our enemy the devil as I counseled with Mary. Following a tearful, distressing phone call from her, I offered to come to her home, bringing also one of our other pastors. The three of us sat together in Mary's front room while her husband tended the baby in a back room.

Significant revelations of Mary's past came out. She had been deeply involved in occult practices, to the extent of leading séances in the cemetery. My associate and I prayed then and there for her release, and I urged her to vocalize her own prayer of full surrender.

Suddenly, she shrieked loudly and fell to the floor on all fours. At this, the baby awakened and cried out, and her husband came running. I met him in the hall and assured him, "Bill, I know what is wrong. Please trust me and take the baby for a walk. Mary will be OK." Remarkably, he turned and went outside, carrying the crying child for a walk.

Mary was a sight, leaning forward on her knees with both saliva and mucus streaming down, crying and groaning. She tried unsuccessfully to follow my directions to her to confess Jesus as Lord. Every attempt to form the word "Jesus" failed. Only the sound "J . . . J" came out.

Since Mary was a professing Christian, I wanted her volition to be fully active in this encounter, rather than my doing something for her or to her. However, Satan's challenge had to be met, so I commanded the enemy in Jesus' name to depart from her at once. Mary then prayed with freedom her own prayer of victory and release.

Later on her husband and young son joined her in the faith.

A series of incidents showing God's providence brought a member of an internationally famous singing group—the American version of the Beatles—to our church. He readily accepted my invitation to dinner, and while the meal was being prepared, we sat under a tree in our back yard. He said that he was guitarist, vocal soloist, and songwriter for his band. I learned also that he was on his way to national exposure on a Christian TV program. Hearing this and surmising that this Christian program director was about to yank into premature exposure a spiritual embryo that was not yet viable, I jarred him with this warning: "Like a hole in the head you need public exposure of what you think God is doing in your life—you are still infected with demons!" I said this because of what I discerned from the experiences he was sharing with me that afternoon.

Nevertheless, he plowed ahead with his plans, and he indeed fell back into his old ways. For a while I lost touch with him, until his wife turned up in church again, a broken and confused woman. But God had mercy and later brought him back to our church, much humbled and very contrite. Ultimately both he and his wife became useful servants of Christ together in a local church.

During the late 1960s and 1970s churches everywhere were suffering black eyes for being out of touch with youth. Many churches adopted the style of the streets in an effort bridge the cultural gulf between church and young people. I was not impressed with this approach and determined that, rather than making changes, we ought to sharpen what we were doing while seeking new power from God. This worked, and our children and youth ministries flourished. We gave special attention to parents, helping them to lead their families and not to lean unduly on the church to provide all their kids' teaching and entertainment.

At one point an entire company of street young people, traveling down our highway from the famous 1969 Woodstock Festival, stopped in the offices to check out our church. In surprising frankness they admitted dissatisfaction with the street scene. "We didn't see the love everyone spoke of. We saw selfishness instead." Their outpouring went even further, concluding, "We want to get back into the mainstream. Can you help?"

My reply: "That will require your coming under authority. If you are willing for that, you have come to the right place. Our church is an entire fellowship of love, under authority." They stayed with us.

First, I insisted that any thefts and the like had to be made right. Some went to area service stations to repay robberies they had committed. An out-of-wedlock baby with severe abnormalities (only one half of its head) died at birth, leaving the parents in distress. I was able to offer some hours of pastoral help to them.

During this same period I was invited to be interviewed by a seminary class. What I feared might await me occurred. The students sat around the classroom on the floor, not in chairs.

The professor wore his long hair in the style of the youth, a large bronze cross dangled from his neck, and he labored to speak in contemporary style.

Then it began, with the professor leading the attack, "Pastor, does not all the inequities of suffering and needy ones in our society grieve and hurt you?"

"Yes, it does hurt."

"Where do you feel it?"

I patted my chest over my heart and said, "Right here!"

All the students then launched into their attack. "What's wrong with the church today—it's so uncaring and out of touch!" On and on they went.

That did it! I was not going to sit by and allow their broad-brush maligning of our Lord's body, so I stopped them in their tracks with this: "I listened to you; now please hear me. Let me tell you what I'm doing these very days." I proceeded to tell them of the youth off the streets that were coming to us and of all the care and healing they were receiving. Then I told them of the last thing I did before leaving town to drive to their class: "I went to a widow's home with four or five children, some of whom are deeply troubled youngsters and need much attention from other families of the church. That's what I do. What do you do?" Mostly silence.

Needs of modern youth are many and deep. On another occasion immediately following my message in a Christian college chapel service, one of the several hundred students came up on the platform to talk with me. He was choking with sobs, so I took him aside to an office and sent word to the dean to come directly because I sensed that this was an emergency. It was indeed serious. He confessed that he was guilty of armed robbery.

75

After counsel and prayer, he was definitely at peace. We arranged for his immediate departure from school to return home, face the police, and make restitution to the drugstore he had robbed.

Truly amazing results came with every step he took. First, he went to the victimized store clerks. In awe, they heard his confession and looked in the face of the one who wore the mask, covering his boyish face. "I returned the money, and they forgave me," he happily recounted to me. "Next, I went to the beach hangout where my buddy was sure to be, and there he was. I simply told what I had done to make things right and announced that I was going to turn myself in to the police and admit what both of us had done. Then I went to the police, confessing that I was the masked robber. When they heard that I'd already faced the store and returned my part of the stolen cash, they also forgave me and dropped the charges." Eventually, the young man went out as a missionary and served in a foreign field for many years.

An earlier episode working with Boston's inner-city youth perhaps taught me as much as they might have learned from me. I became sick with a significant fever and nausea some hours ahead of the evening appointment, where I was to speak to the several hundred teenagers. Rising from bed, I took my Bible in hand and wobbled out to the back seat of my car. A friend drove me to the appointment in the city. For some reason I felt drawn to preach on a very heavy doctrinal theme. "What was I thinking to choose this text for an inner-city crowd of rowdy, unchurched young people?" I asked myself.

When I was introduced, it sounded to me as though the speaker was calling to me from a great distance. Mechanically, I walked to the podium and held myself steady with one hand, gripping the back of the stand. But as I spoke (and the message was centered on Christ's blood-offering in payment for our sin), God taught me a lesson I've always remembered. Strength is more of a hindrance than weakness when one is utterly cast upon the Holy Spirit.

The teens were quiet, and the Spirit worked powerfully. My effort to have repentant ones come to the front proved futile, because so many were pressing down the clogged aisles. No room remained across the entire front. All three aisles also began filling.

Hospitals have ever been a fruitful field for work and witness. I made it a practice to enter these institutions through the emergency ward. Over the years I have had many special encounters there.

God's preparation and answer to prayer is the only explanation for events like the brief story I now relate. It was a four-bed ward, and I was speaking to a rough man I had never met before. He was obviously in significant pain from an earlier hernia surgery. After he thought soberly over my Gospel challenge, he suddenly burst out in a loud voice to the other men of the ward, "Hey, you guys, listen to this man. Hear what he is telling me. We all need this!" We had a special encounter that evening.

Like experienced fishermen, we need to go where the fish are. Thus I sometimes went into bars to bear testimony to the Gospel. Patrons were usually willing to listen. Not counting those in a stupor, there were some who gave alert attention.

Once I went looking for the husband and father of a church family. There he was in his favorite bar. On the way to his table I passed another man attending our church who was parked on a bar stool looking right toward me. His eyes widened in total surprise, and he spun around on his stool in a futile effort to escape my notice. Standing over my seated friend at the table, I could see that he was already half-drunk, and his hand held a half-filled bottle. On hearing me call his name, he looked up into the face of his pastor and gasped. I asked, "Are you willing to come with me so I can talk with you?" Without complaint, he obediently pushed back from the table and followed me into the hallway.

When I informed him that his wife was at that moment packing to leave him and return to her parents in another state, he stumbled out of the bar and entered my car. Suddenly he burst into uncontrollable weeping and shouted, "Pull over! Pull over!" Pouring out his heart in prayer, he pled for forgiveness from God and placed himself before the cross as his only hope.

This began a complete and permanent turnaround for the entire family. His wife realized the change in her husband and returned to him with all her heart. He then brought his children to me to find salvation and help with their problems. Ultimately, all the family, including the children, became very helpful leaders in the church.

A frantic phone call began a whole series of dramatic events one afternoon. The call came from a home just a few miles from my church office. I begin the story here, quoting directly from my book *Bringing Christ Back*.

> Ben was desperate. He instinctively drove to the home of his friends Tom and Mary. Mary was shocked at his appearance and even more disturbed at his words. "Drinking has finally caught up to me. I'm ruined . . . nothing to live for . . . lost my job. Sonya has packed

up and left with the kids. I can't handle things any more . . . falling to pieces!"

Seeing him trembling and hinting of taking his life sent Mary in a panic to the Yellow Pages in search of a church that might help. Though she was Catholic, out of deference to her Southern Protestant friend, she looked for one of his kind. That is how she happened to dial my church.

"Are you the 'father' of the church?" she blurted out. "Our friend Ben here is falling apart. Drinking and living it up has ruined him and his home. I'm afraid he's having a breakdown right here and now! Can you help?"

Ben managed to drive his sports car to the church office, and in walked what was once a handsome thirty-five-year-old man of the world. Now he was too distraught even to relate his story. Seeing he was so near the edge, I decided on an emergency approach.

"Ben, do you believe in the Lord Jesus Christ?" His answer was delivered in short, painful gasps of speech: "Yes, I'm saved . . . at my home church in Texas. I know about the Holy Ghost, too . . . but now I need help!" His words ended in a pleading wail. With eyes closed and head lowered, a trembling hand signaled that he could talk no further. He was sinking, and there was not a moment to lose.

I felt I must somehow arouse him to take hold of truth, but I had two difficult questions to face: What truth should I use? and How might I possibly get it over to him? What would you do to help this struggling, fainting man?

Breathing a short prayer, I jolted him with a question, causing his eyes to open and his head to lift. "Ben, here is a question maybe you haven't heard before: Where was Jesus before he was conceived in his mother's womb? (Please, keep your head up for a moment!) I didn't exist before my mother conceived me, nor did you. Was it any different with Jesus?

Grimacing, he groaned out this response, "I don't know . . . never even thought of that. I reckon not."

Now I had discovered a truth he was missing and sorely needed. Just as I had sensed from the outset, his earlier spiritual experience had seemed real to him, but it was no match for the temptations that had dragged him into his present state.

With a burst of genuine excitement, I spoke more loudly, "There's your problem, Ben! Maybe now I can help. You've got the wrong Jesus!" As his eyes met mine with a questioning examination, I added quietly, "That Jesus you described does not exist."

Now he was bolt upright. With eyes wide open, he stammered, "What . . . what do you mean?"

Into that gaping heart, I poured in truth, in simple and brief sentences, explaining that the One who was eternal God stooped to the door of the womb to enter our world. I referred to John 1:14: the Son "became flesh and made his dwelling among us. We have seen his glory, the glory of the One and Only, who came from the Father, full of grace and truth."

"Ben, God himself came in human form and suffered on the cross for the very sin that is destroying you. But Jesus did not stay dead. He is now alive to hear and help you—right now." In a moment we were kneeling at our chairs there in my study. His prayer was earnest, honest, and offered with mounting hope.

Before I give the remarkable conclusion to our story, let me interject a defense for my "unprofessional" procedure. I am well aware of the standard rules for counseling that I appeared to break on that afternoon years back. I sensed at once, however, that Ben thought of himself as a believer in Christ and as one who held the Bible's teachings. To me, though, he looked rather like a woodsman inching his way out on an unsound limb. The further he went, the more certain his fall was becoming.

The limb of truth on which many begin their climb in life may not be very strong and sound. It is important, therefore, that we all gain more solid doctrinal support as we get on in our spiritual lives. Misconceptions regarding major truths will not support the weight of life's heavier trials. That was Ben's jeopardy. Attempting to relieve his troubled mind would not be enough. He was dangling over disaster from a belief system that was inadequate and cracking under the weight of his problems. I went there first, knowing that a spiritual renewal would make it easier to get him through to God's help. Here is what happened.

As we arose from our prayer, Ben was no longer agitated and shaking. His eyes were wide open, and he was able to converse with me more normally. "When did you last eat?" I asked. As I suspected, he had not been eating properly, so I phoned ahead to

Jane to say that I was bringing a new friend home to dinner. Once we were in our home, my good wife, sensing the situation, put him entirely at ease and drew a smile from him.

As the meal progressed, Ben's transformation continued. Now he was relishing the opportunity to talk about his wife, Sonya, and the children. With mounting hope, he mused, "If only I could get her to come and talk to you."

The next morning the stylish, attractive young mother and wife sat in my office. Already she was convinced that some significant change had come into Ben's life, and she wanted to know what this was. Early in our interview, she admitted her own personal need to find peace with God and readily accepted the invitation to repent and turn in faith to Jesus Christ. Later that very day the family was reunited and returned to their home.

Seeing the strength of their new commitment to the Lord and to one another, I gave them a special challenge. "Apparently your home is a gathering place for a number of couples who are special friends. Why not gather them for a different kind of 'party'? Tell them what new things Christ has done for you, and then begin a weekly Bible study."

With enthusiasm the invitation went out to a number of couples who filled their living room to hear Ben and Sonya's story and to hear one of the men from our church teach them gospel truth. In time, nearly all of them became committed believers, including Mary, the friend who had originally phoned about Ben's need. (146–49)

Chapter 12

God at Work on the University Campus

We carried our church's witness directly to the university campus in several ways. All members of the church who attended area schools of higher learning were encouraged and helped to bear Christian testimony in the class sessions, interactions with fellow students, and even discussions with their professors. Once a week several specially prepared young men and women went into the dorms; Bible studies often resulted.

One professor who chaired a department at the state university was known for his direct assaults on positions held by students who believed in Christ and the veracity of Scripture. An older, mature student asked me how he might give an effective rebuttal. We talked together and came up with a plan, which he set in motion when the next attack came.

Raising his hand for permission to speak, he laid down a challenge before the class to his professor. "Sir, since this is a place of higher learning, we ought to hear the other side put by one who is trained as you are, and then we can make our own decisions in these matters. And I know such a man who would be willing to come to do this."

The professor did not allow me to attend a class, but he did agree to bring two carloads of students to a restaurant for lunch and debate. I'm sure no one who was there that day remembers what we ate! My opponent was brilliant and more consistent in his agnosticism than I ever expected.

I finally said, "So if I massaged your scalp with a crowbar, you would want justice, even though you argue that there is no essential spirit in a man, only blank matter. Choice is all preprogrammed into each person from his genes and conditioning—is that what you are saying?"

"Exactly," he agreed.

"Thus you argue your case as an atheist, but you would cry for justice as if you were a theist." Nothing moved him.

Nothing, that is, until we stood on the sidewalk outside the restaurant, where I commented, "It's surprising how different things are at your school here from the large university in the South where my brother serves as a dean. Professors and leaders I have met there are solid church members and believers, and they value the Bible."

"That may be true. I and my colleagues, though, wouldn't hold a job five minutes in those schools."

Just what I wanted that circle of eager ears to hear! "Yes, but do you admit that to your students? Or do you lead them to feel that your position is that of all truly thinking people?"

I was invited to one of the frat houses for a debate. This came about at the initiative of their chef, who was a loyal member at our church. In his typical blunt style, he responded to their good-humored taunts about his simple faith with a challenge: "You guys throw big words around, but you need to listen to someone who can answer and silence you. And I know one who can do it—my pastor!"

At that, they invited me to a Sunday lunch with them. While I ate, most of them sat listening in, while two or three led the charge against basic Christianity. I listened quietly, responding here and there until I felt the time was right for me to speak up. "I have listened all this time to you, and now I ask you to hear me thoughtfully. What evidence do you have for the positions you are taking?" This question was greeted with silence, so I pressed it further. "Surely, if you are going to cast Christianity aside and go out on all these limbs, you must have proof."

Right then, one of the fellows called out to their leading spokesman, "Yeah, Joe! What proof have we? We don't even agree with each other!" All laughed at this quandary.

I followed up with a simple, coherent statement of the Christian faith and Gospel. I was late for our evening service but had prepared for the eventuality, and I felt it was well worth the cost.

A special and powerful work among university students began with a young chemist. He was well into his Ph.D. program when he attended one of our church services and raised his hand, indicating that he wished prayer for himself. I invited him to our home for discussion and fellowship, and thus began a spiritual saga that continues until this day, a half-century later.

Very soon, Ron made plans to drop his much loved science studies and transfer to seminary. To be expected was the immediate visit of his concerned parents. What had happened to their boy? The father was a known banker from a nearby state. (This was only one of several such visits I have received over the years).

Ron readily agreed to my suggestion to call all his friends together for a discussion. Because the private home he rented was a gathering place for students who liked his free tutoring, a large group filled his living room on the appointed evening. The lively discussion went on until early morning. All of those attending were graduate students, with some in their doctoral studies. Several nationalities were present. The gist of our meeting went something like this: first, I received quietly their stored-up challenges to the Christian faith. Then I quieted them with my regular tactic, "I listened to you, now you listen to me, please!" To disarm and deflate them a bit, I proceeded in this way: "Since you seem very negative toward my view of the Bible, it is very important that you tell me what you think my view of Scripture is." As I suspected, they could not adequately define the point of view that they were assailing.

"You think God told Moses and others what they had to write down."

"So you believe that I think God more or less dictated the words, somehow making his voice heard so they could write down the book I have here in my hand. Is that what you think I hold to?" Yes, they were in general agreement that this was my position. Then I shocked them with the words, "Well, we finally are agreed on something! Along with you, I reject that view. In fact, I have never met anyone who held it. It is a basic axiom in intellectual discussion that one must be able to correctly state the position that one is trying to overturn. Yet you have jettisoned Scripture without even knowing what Christians actually think of it."

After this exchange I had a much more receptive audience. Before our wee-hour conclusion, I issued this appeal, "Consider what you have lost if you one day face God and discover what I've said is true. But what have I lost, even if you are right?" I proceeded directly to present the atonement through Christ, making it very clear how one may be right in the sight of God and escape holy judgment.

A second such meeting was also held, and by then some fruit was beginning to emerge. As I recall, at least two of the group became ministers of the Gospel, and definitely all were impacted.

Andy, the most recalcitrant individual of the group, the one who was most aggressive in his verbal assaults, abruptly stopped coming and sent a curious written note to me after I had given him the following challenge: "Andy, you speak as if you are a thoroughgoing materialist—but are you really? Look at that wooden coffee table in front of you. Don't you know instinctively that you are qualitatively different from that piece of wood? Don't you sense that my words are not just mechanical bumping of atoms? Don't you sense that God himself is looking in on this meeting and is trying to get a hearing from you?"

His note, written in blank verse, related the strange story of a lone, struggling figure in utter darkness, stumbling along a mountain pass, heading toward his ultimate destiny, over an abyss into eternal blackness. Suddenly, for the first time in his life, he sees a faint glimmer of light approaching him. It's a firefly! Cupping it in his hands, the weary traveler falls to his knees in tears and utter delight. At last he has seen some light! Alas, the firefly escapes through his fingers and sails away out over the abyss, disappearing forever. The pitiful pilgrim struggles to his feet and trudges on toward the dark abyss that surely awaits him.

Both Ron and I agreed on the interpretation. Andy knew he was a pilgrim in darkness, going he knew not where, but one day he has an encounter with the light of some truth. This meant that I was the firefly, but his initial elation was not to last. He was one destined for doom. Nothing worked to restore any communication with him.

At this writing, my friend Ron has logged many years as a faithful pastor and preacher of God's truth. Only a few days ago he sent me a loving expression of appreciation that he has now had fifty years as a believer in God's family.

"Your sermon made me so angry! I don't know why I didn't just get up and walk out of here!" That was the greeting at the church door given by Emily, an irate young woman who had just heard my message on the Christian family, emphasizing instructing and training our sons and daughters. It turned out that she was in the nearby university's psychology department, working as a teaching assistant while continuing her own doctoral studies in psychology and counseling.

"I have a suggestion. Why not get together with me so I can understand your views and share mine with you? Please come to my house for a dinner, and then we can more completely talk things over in my study." I did this partly to expose her to my family of four young children, and then she could better see for herself how things were.

While she stammered and hesitated—but without refusing—her friend who had brought her to church said excitedly, "Yes, Emily, that would be a great idea. I'll go with you."

"All right," she said with grudging hesitancy.

The big night arrived, and the three of us sat chatting in our front room while Jane finished meal preparations and our four children played quietly within sight of the guest. Sometimes they were in and out of my lap or excused themselves as they asked a question, and they did little things that made our guest feel at ease. As we sat at the table, I mentioned our regular practice of prayer before eating, then said, "Tonight, family, let's have two of you pray for our meal." Without hesitancy, the two whose names I called, offered sincere prayers, and as was our custom, they included the guest in their thanksgiving.

Following dinner, I invited Emily to come across the hall to my study. As she arose to follow me out, she said loud enough for my wife and her friend to hear, "You're going to hate me when I say what I am going to say." Though that was surely not what I wanted to hear, I was glad that my wife and the friend could be more urgent in their prayers while we were meeting. We sat down opposite one another by the desk, and at once I interjected, "I always like to pray before a conversation like this." Without waiting for her response, I began the prayer, acknowledging Jesus Christ, his person and work, and imploring (and I do mean imploring!) God for his help in our discussion. Raising my head, I looked squarely at her and waited for her opening words, which I will never forget:

"Well . . . I guess . . . I'm just lost!" My heart overflowed with secret praise as I proceeded to point her to the Savior. She agreed to seek the Lord through his Word and give him opportunity to speak to her. Thus ended our first meeting.

Emily left directly, and as my wife closed the door behind Emily, she confronted me with an expression of utter amazement. "What happened to her? Her very countenance is changed!"

Changed indeed—by the power of God. Back to the campus she went with her Bible in her hand and Christ in her life. On one occasion, she returned to her desk in the Psych Department to discover that someone had taken her Bible from her desk and dumped it in the wastebasket. Other incidents also occurred, as she experienced the same demonic outbursts against her that she had once leveled at me. My last contact with her some years later disclosed that she was serving Christ as a Christian counselor.

The Holy Spirit's blessing was apparent from beginning to end in an encounter with the Pharmacy Department of the nearby state university. Soon after I met the department professor, she read my book *Last Light*, which details the journey of my wife and me through the first ten years of her Alzheimer's disease.[2] This professor then arranged for all her fifth-year students to read the book. As a follow-up, I was invited to address these students.

It was a moving and powerful session. I present excerpts here from a few of their written reactions to the lecture, sent to me by the professor.

> I know what drives me and what makes me happy, sad, excited—but all of that seems so insignificant in comparison with this type of situation. I may be happy or sad about a grade, but in this perspective it helps me learn that, while important, school and grades aren't everything.

> In class he told us that, after everything, he believed that she was more beautiful after the sixty years of marriage than when he married her. I hope that one day I'll be as lucky as Jane to have someone to be willing to do that all for me and that I'll be as patient as Harold, if it comes down to it.

> I thought my problems actually mattered until I heard about someone who watched the love of his life fall apart both mentally and physically, and I realized sometimes we all need a reality check.

> How he was able to push himself to such lengths and still manage to care for his wife in such a complete

---

[2] Harold Burchett, *Last Light: Staying True through the Darkness of Alzheimer's* (Colorado Springs: NavPress, 2002).

and loving manner is beyond fathomable. He credits the Lord, his friends, and his family in supporting him and his wife. I not only hope that I may have such a deep and loving relationship . . . but also such a support group to help my in the most trying of times.

I enjoyed Dr. Burchett's visit because it gave us new insight into the care of Alzheimer's. It was touching to see how much he cared for his wife throughout the twenty years he spent taking care of her and her disease. It was also interesting to read in the article what a huge role God played in his life. He is a very spiritual man, and it was nice to learn about his wife and how she fit into his life before the disease set in.

He devoted his life to the promise he kept to his wife. He mentally, physically, and spiritually poured every last ounce of fight he had into her and did so with grace. He exemplified what it means to live honestly and passionately.

If you looked into this man's eyes when he was speaking about his wife, you would understand. He spoke with an unconditional love and peacefulness in each word.

I will never forget his story and how it taught me that we all have an inner strength to overcome tremendous odds. I think it also reinforced an old saying that "love conquers all," whether that be love of another person, love of God, or both.

After collecting and reading all the reports, the professor wrote these words to her students, "Thank you for your comments. I agree completely. I've spoken with him many times, and read his book . . . but the way he tells the stories and his positive attitude . . . it just amazes me. It does make you think about the big picture and gives a different meaning to 'for better or for worse.'"

Finally, I relate an encounter with academia of a decidedly different tone. When I was a student at a Christian college, I made some good contacts in the student body of a nearby teacher's college. Somehow I gathered a few of the students to sing favorite hymns during lunch break. It proved to be so popular that we had to move to the gymnasium, where the walls shook with our enthusiastic singing. For a while one could almost forget that this was *not* a Christian institution. The expected word from the officials came, and I gave up my noon rallies.

Six or eight of the young women, however, invited me to have a home discussion meeting. In answering their questions, I decided against a dry intellectual approach. Before long, I said with all my heart, "You're asking me how I can be so sure even of God's existence. That's simple: because I *know* him! In fact, I was talking with him only this morning!" As I recall, these contacts from long ago led to lasting fruit.

Chapter 13

Things That Went Wrong—Apparently

Accurate telling of such spiritual warfare as I am attempting to recount requires that I frankly admit painful reverses. But being knocked down does not necessarily mean being knocked out in defeat, as the following stories will show.

"You've destroyed us!" This outcry was not exactly what I wished for when I invited public response after the last sermon in a series of meetings in a neighboring church. I had made the point that, before teaching another's children, one ought to have one's own house in order. Two teachers rose to their feet in response to my admonition, and both resigned publicly, on the spot. This brought an outburst from the Sunday School superintendent indicating that I had destroyed their work.

Somehow amid the crosscurrents of feelings, I nevertheless felt that the Holy Spirit had been at work that week. This was somewhat confirmed by the pastor, who came to me right after the service and said with deep conviction, "Regardless of what anyone says, God has truly worked in my life these days, and it will continue."

And so it turned out. That very summer the Sunday School not only was not "destroyed" but had doubled in size, and the church had built a small educational wing. Such experiences reassured me that God's ways sometimes carry us upstream against popular feelings. I can further confirm the fruit of these meetings. Only recently—several decades after hearing this outcry—I met a man and his wife who asked me if I remembered preaching that series of messages. "I do," I replied, and then they told me that their own conversion stemmed from that series. Someone converted in that early day had brought the Gospel to several others, including to them.

Here was one angry pastor! Some of his own church people had gotten converted as I preached, so he threatened, "If any are 'saved,' I'll get them unsaved!" He set about to do exactly that, going from house to house on his mission.

His fury was first kindled when a group of women asked his permission to have evening services. Permission was granted by the pastor, providing that they took care of everything and he was not burdened with their vision. I was one of the first guest speakers for this strange arrangement. I arrived at the church and was met only by one of the ladies. Our service was well attended, however, and there, sitting near the back, was the pastor and his wife. As far as I know, there was no evangelical church of any kind in the town, and the service that day included representatives of very liberal churches. I managed, however, to get the congregation to sing Gospel songs with gusto.

At one point I noticed the pastor's wife abruptly walk out of the service. He stayed on and witnessed a large number of people respond to a public invitation for sinners to repent and confess Christ. This is what infuriated him the most, it seems. He never spoke to me from the time I arrived until I left.

His mission of undoing this work of God evidently came to naught. A new church immediately sprang up from the converts and became a thriving work for God.

Kit was only twelve or thirteen years of age and appeared to be about eleven when she stood trembling before the judge. A sheriff had told me of her tragedy-filled life, so I made sure I was present in the courtroom to witness this moment. Here is her story. She had just borne a child by her own father. He went to state prison, and I had worked with the authorities to have the baby adopted into a distant Christian home. Kit then became a charge of the state. Officials seemed not to know what to do with her—hence this hearing before the judge. It was a private hearing, and I was the only one there besides the police, the judge, and poor Kit. As soon as the judge disclosed that he was considering sending her to a reform school, my sense of justice rose up in protest. Gaining permission to speak privately to the judge, I said, "She has not violated the law. She herself has *been* violated. Therefore, why is she going to be sent to reform school?"

"We have no other place for a youngster of her age and situation. What do you suggest?"

"What if I take her into my home?" I inquired.

"That would be fine," he replied, "but can you handle this?"

I asked for two things. First, that he make Kit aware of this plan, and second, that the choice could be hers after she visited my home for a look. She could choose the reform school instead if that was her desire. Then I asked for permission to drive her straight to my home and broach (or should I say, spring?!) the matter with my wife.

Without any warning, the two of us walked in on my Jane. Without batting an eye, she kindly received the struggling youngster (in so many ways still a child) and showed her around the house. "I think I'd rather live here," she said.

We drove directly back to the judge's office, and he assigned her to us. This began a decidedly new era in her life and, I must

95

add, new for my family also. Kit was intrigued with our habit of evening Bible study and prayer. Bible lessons for her had to be made much simpler than for my own younger children. One of the problems we encountered was her basic, lifelong dishonesty. She seemed genuine in her desire to get rid of this habit, but still she would compulsively take things around the house and store them under her mattress.

Another problem showed its frowning face when the state social worker in charge of her case came to our house to make sure that Kit was not wrongly indoctrinated with my Christian beliefs.

After two years, Kit no longer oscillated back and forth between adulthood and childhood. She was becoming an attractive young woman and seemed to like our church fellowship—that is, until the day she met a tough-looking young man astride a motorcycle. I learned of this the hard way when she did not come home one evening. I located her on the streets and had an opportunity to make a final appeal to her, "Kit, see how God has blessed you. Just look at you, how different and new you are becoming. You can be a beautiful woman of God!" The biker sat a short distance away, perhaps within earshot. Kit looked pitifully into my face and then back at the biker. Then, without a word to me, she turned and went to climb on the machine with him. They rode away into the night, and I never saw her again. It was heartbreaking.

"Harold, I've been fired!" These words in the telephone shook my groggy mind one midnight. Let me tell you the story. Mainly at the pastor's initiative, I was invited to conduct a series of evangelistic meetings at a church in a village close by the city where I pastored. The pastor himself was unique in his personality and life. Basically, in addition to being an earnest believer, he was a philosopher. He lived and thought in abstractions. At least he did until God started a striking new work in his spiritual life. He went almost to the opposite extreme, now being pressed in his spirit to take up pastoring in this little church. He was ceaseless in going into the homes of his members, warning and pleading with people to be saved. Most of the old guard in the church were shocked and alarmed and struggled to resist his urgings.

A considerable number of the members, however, were deeply stirred, and a loyal band of newly converted shipyard workers gathered around him and held a weekly meeting beseeching God's blessing on their church. That's where I came into the picture. After much prayer and deliberation, they decided to seek my help as an evangelist to turn the very liberal church congregation toward the Lord Jesus Christ and personal salvation.

A collision between heaven and hell took place during the last service of the series, held on a Sunday night. Throughout the service there was a peculiar restlessness among my hearers, with constant shuffling and scuffling of feet, stirring in the seats, and coughing—an eerie atmosphere. Only eight or nine people responded to the public invitation, but I strongly felt that the entire congregation needed to be on their faces before God. I therefore announced that I would not dismiss the service but would rather end the preaching and leave open God's call to salvation. "Jane will be at the piano, singing 'Lord, I'm Coming Home.' As you rise from your seats and step into aisle, make a choice whether you will come to the front and join these here who will be kneeling in prayer, or whether, if you do not choose the Savior, you will turn and go out lost from him."

With that, I walked down from the pulpit and made my way out the aisle where people were standing, hesitating in thought. Then, as if a divine broom had swept down each aisle, nearly all of them turned and came to the front. I continued to the back and prevailed on several more to return inside. Coming back to the front of the church, an amazing scene greeted me. People were on their knees from one side of the church to the other, several rows deep. It was a solid mass of kneeling, repentant people weeping and praying aloud one after another. A Roman Catholic organist who was paid for his weekly services sat in wide-eyed amazement, viewing the scene but unable to step down from his bench. He was completely surrounded by people on their knees praying to God. I don't remember much more of these happenings until the pastor's phone call woke me some nights later. His words "I'm fired!" were quite a surprise. It seemed like an "end" but perhaps it was a new and true beginning.

Here's the rest of the story. The few who rejected the Spirit's work set about to get rid of the pastor. Since it was a congregationally run church of the old New England parish system, members of the surrounding community were free to vote. All kinds of outsiders were pressed to attend the decisive meeting, and they managed enough votes to override the faithful. As an added incentive to hasten the pastor's departure from their midst, the old guard leaders disconnected the electrical service to the parsonage, leaving the pastor and his little family without even refrigeration. He was broken hearted but firm in his faith.

Driven to do something that would sustain their spiritual life, all the men and women who now openly confessed their faith in the Savior, left en masse and built another church meeting place. They thrived, and the other group shriveled.

"This is not what I paid for!" Such was the negative appraisal of my ministry at a Christian summer conference center. The picturesque surroundings were both beautiful and restful, but my messages had been too searching for some. The director also voiced his concern. I understood but was not convinced.

The tension was evident at a morning Bible Study when I stated that Christians who truly are among God's saved ones will not continue in the practice of sin. This brought up the plea not to forget eternal security, which I affirmed, even while insisting that no doctrinal viewpoint must give a sense of safety and security for sin. When the complaints continued, I warned that safe sin was not prescribed in Scripture. Then, looking at the group of seasoned believers, I challenged them, "I have heard your plea for the right to sin in safety. But now does anyone have a word for holiness?" It was quiet.

Another deeply convicting moment that week came at an evening service when I reported the results of an unsigned survey I had given all of them. It was a self-inventory consisting of a series of very personal questions meant to expose one's spiritual life. All questions were to be answered unequivocally, Yes or No. For example:

Yes___ No___	I am now reading daily in the Bible.
Yes___ No___	I understand what the filling of the Holy Spirit means.
Yes___ No___	I believe that I now have the fullness of the Spirit.
Yes___ No___	I know of at least one continuing sin in my life over which I cannot seem to get victory.
Yes___ No___	I am a genuine believer in Christ and feel certain that I am saved.

Almost everybody returned their completed forms, and I promised to announce the results the next night. If a person's responses were contradictory—for example, saying Yes both to "I believe that I now have the fullness of the Spirit" and to "I know of at least one continuing sin in my life over which I cannot seem to get victory"—I discounted that paper as contradictory.

The next night the tabernacle was well filled with interested people. I announced the results of the survey: "I can count on the fingers of one hand those of you who have a consistent certainty of their salvation in Christ. We badly need a spiritual awakening!" That night the Word of God spoke powerfully to many hearts.

Even though I did not give invitations for a public display of commitment, I recall that there was significant evidence of God's working. People sought me out for prayer and counsel. The first one who came to our cottage was a pastor's wife who admitted sorrowfully to me that she herself had never been really converted. She went home, I sincerely believe, a new woman, gladdening the heart of her husband. Another one I helped, a woman with deep personal needs, was the superintendent of an active Sunday School.

"I can't give him up!"—words that all but broke my heart to hear. I had gotten Edna to come to my study for an urgent interview. She was involved with another man, much to the grief of her husband and three young children. In an effort to shake her loose from her intoxicating bewitchment, I proceeded to bring her children before her—not physically, but by using graphic word descriptions. As I concluded with my word picture of the youngest, a sweet, beautiful, blue-eyed child of two who wore long blond curls over her shoulders, Edna was visibly shaken and weeping. But she pled for more time to "think."

"Edna, what is there to think about? See those children! Will their mother give them up and choose adultery instead?"

"I know, Pastor (sobbing and groans), but I must go now. I promise to call you."

"Oh, Edna, if you walk out that door, I fear you are turning your back on your children and your God. Do not do that." Nothing would stop her hasty exit. She literally fled from me.

A day later she called and choked out her answer, "Pastor, I can't give him up!"

Another negative outburst occurred one Sunday night following my evening message. As I went down from the pulpit and stationed myself in front of the Communion table, a very angry man came steaming down the center aisle and confronted me in a rage. He was bothered by my call to an unequivocal quitting of sin and the need to live a holy life—or else give up dogmatic certainty of salvation. I felt I had to quiet this explosion because other people would obviously become involved. My good intentions were at first ineffective, so I took hold of his arms, gripping one with each of my hands. Holding him tightly, I began to pray aloud, "O Father, help this man who has an angry, mean spirit. . . ."

"I haven't got a mean spirit!"

"Yes he has, Lord. He needs your help now." With that, he jerked free of my grasp, wheeled, and fled down the aisle.

One very large category of puzzling reversals in evangelism was first called to my attention by a missionary. She posed a searching riddle to me: "Why is it that our most shining examples of conversion from the sinful, lost community around us tend to fall away from God? No sooner do we write home our letter of encouragement, citing the example of this or that special conversion, than the convert falls. Sometimes we are struggling to win them back before our good-news letter has reached our home church. It seems to be a pattern. What's wrong?"

Two of the most spectacular "conversions" I ever witnessed both fell into this woeful category. The first was a fine looking young man of thirty years of age. He began witnessing at each opportunity. This included his gripping testimonies given in the church fellowship and his participation in our weekly visitation program among area homes. But without warning, he simply disappeared. I never found out what happened.

The second incident involved an entire family led by a man who quit his heavy drinking, which was threatening his family life, and brought his wife and beautiful children into the church. He soon was confronting his old crowd of drinking buddies and began to preach to them. He would taunt his former friends, saying to them, "You are like kangaroos. You go to the bar, stick out your stomach, and say, 'fill 'er up!'"

It was a moving sight when this entire family presented themselves for baptism. All this made it hurt the more when he went back to drinking. I sought to restore him but never felt certain of his life after that.

A number of valuable lessons may be learned from these trying experiences. First, birthing new babies must cause more than a celebration. We must have in place wise and seasoned safeguards to protect the newborn. The premature exposure of those who are still in embryonic form is more likely to prove abortive.

It is important to remember Jesus' teaching about the tares that are placed among the wheat. To serve the devil's purpose, the tares must be embedded among God's wheat. Thus when they turn away, it is more hurtful to Christ's family.

102

Another fact to hold in mind is that the tares must at first resemble the wheat in order to be misleading. It is particularly hurtful to the church if our great enemy the devil can enable his "plants" within God's family to outshine even true believers. Finally, it must be factored into this puzzle that, if people are humanly delighted in praising the newborn and giving them unwarranted attention, these young plants are likely to be less shielded and protected in fervent prayer by the very ones responsible for their care.

Indelibly burned in my heart is the truth that no one is immune to painful stumbles. A church I once pastored was home to a godly, elderly saint. I'm sure nearly everybody, young and old alike, would have designated him as the one most like our Lord Jesus. But this dearly loved man fell. Listen to the story and learn.

Upon his wife's death, he had to resign himself to living in a nearby nursing home. The residents there immediately recognized something different in him and invited him to offer prayer at all their meals. Those in the administration of this large home were happy that he had moved in.

One day, however, they passed on a disturbing warning, informing me that this elderly and somewhat feeble gentleman was being taken advantage of by a younger woman. "We think the world of him, but he is no match for the wiles of this woman," an administrator confided. When I met this temptress, it was apparent that she was not well balanced emotionally and was simply caught up in her scheme of physically possessing this saintly gentleman for herself.

In prayer I presented my case with God, "Surely, O God, you can't give up this dear brother to the clutches of this woman!" I brought the cross of Christ to the Father and pled for the deliverance of my brother. Next, I sat down alone with him and said flatly, "Brother, Satan has his eye on you. This woman is no gift from God. You belong to our church and to me. I won't give you up, and I won't allow you to go on in this relationship. In the name of Christ, I plead with you, end this wrong relationship now."

In humble submission he prayed and did exactly as I had said. With thanksgiving to God, I embraced him, and he died without breaking the hearts of the little children and adults who so admired him.

"So, if you think you are standing firm, be careful that you don't fall!" (1 Cor. 10:12).

Among the number of military personnel from the nearby base was Billy. He confessed Christ, as did so many of his buddies. One day he called me in great desperation, "Pastor, they have me in jail, and I need you to stand with me now!" Here is a summary of his story to me.

"I bought a rifle from a man here on base. I know it was foolish, but I miss hunting so much! I kept the gun under my bed to avoid having it confiscated, but it was discovered during a room inspection. What makes things so serious now is that apparently the gun had been taken from the base armory. I don't know the name of the person I bought it from, and I am all the more a likely suspect in the eyesof the police because I sometimes stand watch in the armory. When my case comes up, could you at least come to the trial and be a character witness for me?"

Obviously, my heart went out to my distraught friend. Somehow, though, I felt cautious, so I answered, "Give me time to pray over this."

A day or so later, the phone rang in early morning. It was Billy again, and he pressed me urgently, "Pastor, they've moved the trial date up, and it's coming up this very morning, but there's still time for you to make it. Please come and help!" I promised to do what I could and headed to the base directly.

No sooner had I walked into the room than the military court was informed that I had arrived. And before I knew what had happened, I was placed under oath. That moment I determined to tell only what I knew, nothing more. Afterward the Army's prosecuting attorney came straight to me and said, "Sir, you are being suckered into something. Be careful. Your man is lying from beginning to end. Don't get into this."

I stayed noncommittal and went back home and prayed, asking God to help me not to be gullible, but also not to fail to stand with a brother in distress. Also I reminded myself of God's wisdom in trying men and in testing their ways.

While praying, a new insight came to me. After I got up from my knees, I reached for the phone and made contact with Billy's defense lawyer, who of course was glad to have me standing with his client. I asked him, "Why did they suddenly spring this hurried up trial on you?"

"What do you mean by 'hurried up'? We've known of this date for the last month!" There—this is how God showed me the truth, right from Billy's own lawyer! Billy was lying to me and sprang it on me in an attempt to keep me from thinking and praying, trying to get me to rush headlong to his aid.

He was ultimately declared guilty and sentenced for his crime. But I had the problem of his association with our church. So I took one of the elders with me and visited the prison. I wanted to do two things: first, rescue Billy from his sin; second, provide a never-to-be-forgotten learning experience for the church leader.

Billy was brought to the visitation room where we were seated. My first words were deadly serious. "Billy, you are a liar. You lied to me repeatedly, and except for God's help to me, you would have dragged me and our church into the mire of your sin." His face blanched, but he protested that I was mistaken and that he was innocent.

Again I said in strong measured tone, "You—are—lying! And I am speaking to you in the name of the Lord Jesus Christ. You must not and cannot lie to him." Finally his head bowed, and he weakly but humbly muttered, "You are right. I stole the gun."

The good side to all of this is that his confession, though forced out of him, at least gave some room for a restorative ministry.

I have in my top bureau drawer a small golden penknife. It has lain there for sixty-four years, making me sad every time I see it. Once when I was in Canada as a visiting evangelist, a young pharmacist came to see me. He was burdened with the sense of his sin but resisted each time I encouraged him to believe in Christ and surrender to God. Finally, I got him to a point of decision and asked him to kneel at his chair while I knelt at mine. After I prayed, I asked him to make his prayer of repentance and confession to God. He said again, "I can't do it." Still on our knees, I looked at him and explained the Gospel in further detail. He closed his eyes again and started to pray. Abruptly he interrupted his own prayer, shaking his head with finality, "I . . . I just cannot do it now." Standing to his feet, he went back to his store. With a heavy heart I walked to a nearby piano and one-fingered the melody of "Almost Persuaded—but Lost."

A day or two later he dropped off the penknife, engraved with my initials, as an expression of his grief and apology. It did not at all help my hurt, and it remains in the drawer as a reminder of our spiritual war.

Part 3

God's Work in My Personal Encounters

Chapter 14

Forthrightness, Not Harshness

To head off criticism that my personal dealing with people is perhaps harsh, let me offer this perspective. First, I seek to make my support of hurt, troubled, broken people as purposeful as possible—not simply offering a temporary "comfort-fix." Caution must, I think, be exercised in erecting too much supporting scaffolding around the person. Rather than leaning upon ongoing counseling sessions, they must be helped to have personal peace with God and then begin to thrive and progress out of their problems. Still, I must confess to a certain amount of forthrightness, as the following stories will show.

A rather successful salesman I had never met before sat with me in my office. His sister, a member of our church, had urged him to come see me. She was much concerned about him because of his despair over his bondage to drink, to the point that he had talked about taking his own life.

He admitted his dependency on alcohol, so I showed him from the Scripture that his state was indeed sinful. He agreed.

However, when I sought to have him bow in complete repentance and receive Christ's offered blood on the cross, he balked. "Will you now bow with me in prayer and admit to God that you are addicted to drink and claim Christ's blood as payment for your sin and receive his forgiveness? Will you do that?"

After a pause, he said deliberately, "No, I will not."

I knew that nothing I could say would reach him at this point. Yet, I was reluctant to break off things and leave him in that state. So I said quietly, looking him squarely in the eyes, "Here is a remarkable thing: you would rather commit suicide than repent!"

Go for the will, or volition. This is an admonition I follow. Here is another example. Walt was a chain smoker. He had smoked most of his life, and now his health was threatened. "I can't seem to break this habit," he confided. I showed him Romans 6:14: "For sin shall not be your master, because you are not under law, but under grace."

"Notice the two ways of living that are open to you, according to this verse. One, the way of bondage under the law; the other, the way of God's free grace. In the first way, you're on your own, with only your own resources to lean on. But if you choose Christ, he will in grace forgive your sin first, and next he will give you the Spirit of God to help you break free of this tough habit."

"But, Pastor, like I keep telling you, I've smoked since my childhood—all these years! As soon as I walk in the door at work, there are the cigarette machines. And friends will offer smokes to me. I can't just shut this down."

"I understand what you're saying, Walt, but listen carefully. I am not asking you to try that way of escape. God invites you first of all to repent for getting yourself into this bondage and resisting his help. Will you, right this minute, bow before God and admit to him your sin of abusing your body all these years? Then tell God that you don't have the strength to escape this habit, and plead for the help of the Holy Spirit to do what is impossible for you to do." Seeing Walter still hesitating, I repeated yet again, "Will you now do that? Will you?"

"No, I will not," he finally said softly, but with conviction.

"There, Walter, is your true problem. You are not simply unable. You are unwilling. God is able and willing, but you will not choose him and his help." He left unhelped, at least on the surface. Years later, however, I returned to that area. According to my recollection, I found him a free man.

An alcoholic I was striving to help was arrested for drunkenness. I found him in the town jail and paid him a visit. Talking through the bars, I learned that his arrest came about when the police found him in his car, attempting to drive up the railroad tracks.

Characteristically, he began to say that he had learned his lesson and would not again repeat what he had so often repeated. I responded, "You don't know how sorry I am to hear you say that. How I wish you could awaken to the fact that, even though you will be let out of this cell, you will remain hopelessly in prison in your sinful addiction until you fully confess your sin and turn to Jesus in utter helplessness." I do not recall that he ever did so.

An unusual, providential set of circumstances occurred when a pastor friend from a neighboring state came for a visit. We were just returning to my home with some last-minute grocery items when I saw what looked to be a street person standing at my front door—a familiar happening in that city. As I was exiting the car to hear the man's story of need, my friend tugged at my sleeve and whispered, saying, "I know that fellow. I've seen him somewhere . . . I'm trying to think. . . ."

Seated in my study, the man recited his well-worn tale of woe. He explained that he was employed with a carnival and that a series of sad reversals had left him destitute, and now his season of work was over. "I'm just passing through here on my way south, where I will have work." (The "passing-through" status is a familiar explanatory tool used by people of the street to avoid having any prospective donor check up on them.)

"Excuse me for just a moment, friend," I said, as I exited quickly to check with my pastor friend. I asked him, "Have you remembered where you saw this man?"

"Yes, only yesterday he was in our church parking lot [a city south of where I lived] accosting members as they exited from the morning service trying to get money from them."

At that, I wheeled around and returned to my study to confront this dishonest man. "You are lying to me!" I said with considerable force.

"What? No! I'm telling you the truth."

"I know you are a liar because yesterday morning you were south of here in a church parking lot bumming from the members as they came out of the service. God has uncovered your deceit. You had better repent of your sin!"

With that, he jumped to his feet and literally hopped about in his shock, muttering, "Well, if you don't believe a man who tells the truth, I'm going to leave here right now."

"That's right; you are leaving," and I saw him out the front door.

After many, many years of giving counsel and practical help in this particular area of ministry, I have learned that the right blend of persistent love, discernment, and forthrightness is sometimes difficult to find. The local church should be prepared to minister among the community's poor and to conduct ministry in institutions—for example, prisons, even obtaining permission to baptize converted inmates at the church, then training them to become God's witness to other inmates. Help also should be provided in gaining employment for them upon their release.

However, there is no way for a pastor to avoid putting his own hands directly into the soil of this work time and again. As a result, I have endured thefts such as of my own topcoat or other personal effects. Yet through God's help, I have been able to avoid needless waste of gifts upon would-be swindlers. For example, I remember that one stopped midway in his story and asked sheepishly, "I can't lie to you, can I?"

My reply was, "No, and don't try it! Be honest before God; that is first, if you want his help."

Andrew was a successful salesman. When he dropped in at my church office, he was riding high professionally, having just signed a contract involving nation-wide business. His wife, a sincere believer, was probably behind this visit to my study, since Andrew was agnostic.

As soon as he sat down, he began reciting all his agnostic views of one doctrine after another. He declared that it was impossible to know that Christ appeared in actual history, or that he died a special death for our salvation. Furthermore, he especially could not believe the resurrection. After exhausting his immediate negative steam, he sat back and gave me an opportunity to respond. I then prayed aloud very earnestly, but simply, that God would make himself and all that is true clearly known.

I made one other very crucial decision at that very moment. I decided that, since he had so strongly declared from his heart the sum and substance of his unbelief, I ought to declare before him and the surrounding spirit realm the sum and substance of the powerful Gospel.

"Andrew, let me now tell you what I sincerely believe and know to be true." At this point, I simply affirmed my confident faith in each point he had cast down. I could tell he was impacted, though he did not at first admit it. "I understand that you do not now feel free to say this teaching is what you believe, but do you realize that faith is an act of the will? You can choose to believe what God says, and he will help you know the truth, and you will become free through that. The millions and millions of us who believe in Jesus Christ have met him and know him because he is real."

Andrew agreed to take a copy of the New Testament and read the Gospel of John, asking God to help him know and believe. A few days later he returned.

"Have you chosen to believe in Jesus Christ?" I pointedly asked him.

"I am now trying to do that," he said with humble honesty.

"Let's now kneel at our chairs. After I pray, then you tell God you choose to believe in Christ's person and his death and resurrection."

With very strong tones, Andrew almost thundered out his prayer. "O Lord Jesus Christ, I will now believe that you came to earth in a physical body. I choose to believe that your blood is the sacrifice for my sin. I choose to believe that you rose from the dead in a literal resurrection. I want you to be my Lord and my Savior. Amen." A most remarkable prayer indeed!

The next Sunday Andrew not only came to church but stood publicly at the microphone and affirmed the faith he had always doubted. (Public exposure is normally dangerous for new believers, but Andrew, his wife, and I agreed that he ought immediately to make known that he was renouncing his agnostic views and confessing his new faith.)

Blaming God is a popular deception. Ralph had fallen for this deception, though he had never faced it until that day in my study. It became evident when, with sad countenance, he related his story of addiction, starting with alcohol. "You see, God wonderfully delivered me from all desire for alcohol. I'm free of it! Now what troubles me is my addiction to nicotine. I seem unable to quit smoking, but I know God in time will take that from me, just as he did with alcohol."

This deft way of misinterpreting God's grace and resting in it puts the ball wrongfully in God's court. So I first made clear to Ralph the two dimensions of grace:

1. forgiveness and right standing with God through Christ's sacrifice in our place;
2. divine enablement of the Holy Spirit, working in concurrence with our wills for our freedom from sinful practices.

God thus requires his children, who acknowledge what Christ did in their place, to actively choose all that the Spirit waits to do in their heart and life.

Obviously, none of this penetrated, because Ralph repeated his same mournful plea, "But I know I can't do this. God must do it. The flesh is weak."

My response: "Well then, Ralph, let's now bow in prayer and remind God that he must get on the ball and finish what you say he has begun. You pray first!" Complete silence. "Or, Ralph, are you the one in the wrong?"

Blinds of long standing fell from his eyes, and Ralph left that day free. So far as I know, he continued in God's way.

I needed a special touch from God even to get a hearing from this couple. The husband was a bitterly angry man, and the wife, utterly discouraged, was sequestered away in a nearby town. Neither was open to help, and as it turned out, I had but one opportunity to try to talk with each one. I prayed for God's intervention and began with the man.

After listening to a nonstop tirade about his wife's failures and realizing he was not open to reason, I tried this shock approach: "Ephesians 5 clearly says that the man, as head of his wife, is responsible for her spiritual nurture. Therefore, I surely would hate to meet the man who 'headed' his wife into such a disastrous condition as you just described!" He became more subdued and we could more easily talk together.

Before we finished, he told me where his wife was staying temporarily, and I drove there for another kind of confrontation. Phoning her from the apartment lobby, I pled with her to talk with me, since I had driven a considerable distance for the purpose. Reluctantly, she agreed to meet with me, standing there in the lobby.

Realizing that she was not in a trusting mood, I tried desperately to gain her confidence by saying, "I am not representing your husband but only want to help. My hope is that, with help, you might have a new husband in the same skin."

All during this brief encounter, I was praying that God would work two miracles—one to soften her heart, and the other to change her husband. Since the couple were not local residents, I was unable to know what became of their marriage. At least they each could know that someone cared about them and that, if they would let him, God could be their Helper.

Freeing people from the trap of compulsive confessions of sin is a special challenge. Some very earnest Christians are held as prisoners to their own sensitivity. I was talking with one good man who struggled in this way, so I asked him what he did when he sinned during the day.

"I confess the sin, of course."

"When?"

"I always do it immediately, on the spot."

"Then that night before you retire, do you not pray about it again?"

"Yes, I always ask again for forgiveness so I can sleep more peacefully."

"I have a question for you. What Spirit gave us 1 John 1:9, which promises, 'If we confess our sins, he is faithful and just and will forgive us our sins and purify us from all unrighteousness'?"

"God's Spirit inspired all Scripture."

"Then what spirit leads you to doubt what the Holy Spirit has promised, so that you keep reconfessing the same sin?" My friend then bowed his head and asked God to forgive this sin.

An invitation to me was quietly retracted when I frankly questioned my friend. This account was given in my book *Healing for the Church*,[3] from which I quote here:

> A neighboring pastor once invited me to conduct evangelistic services at his church. He went on to explain, "We are small—only about 65 members."
>
> "How many of your members have personally led another person to the Savior?" I asked.

---

[3] Harold Ewing Burchett, *Healing for the Church* (published by the author, 1989).

119

"That is our big problem, and that is precisely why we need you to come and lead the crusade."

"But let us suppose that during our crusade your attendance doubled. You would then have 130 members who would tend to be like one another. What would be the significance of our effort? Are you sure you want more of what you already have?" Arrangements with me for the crusade were dropped at that point. (18–19)

I cannot help but add the comment that this church lacked a realistic plan of edification or discipling. Intense evangelism may gather new bodies into a church, maybe even making it obese, but they will only reproduce in kind, whereas discipling and upbuilding believers will lead them to evangelize.

The power of a single probing question or statement, when spoken under the influence of the Holy Spirit, can change a life forever. Here are two examples:

Dressed in the all-black clothing style of the city streets, the young man poured out one nettling question after another having to do with the Bible. He had just attended his first service in our church, and this is how he greeted me—with questions relating to customs of Bible times and contentious theological issues.

Secretly asking God's help, I interrupted his nervous outpouring with this sobering question: "Are you sure you are asking the question you really *need* to be asking?" (His heart-needs seemed obvious to me!) As our conversation swung to this new, more urgent orientation, he became very serious about his confused life and inadequate, vague notions of God. It was not long before he called upon the Savior he so desperately needed.

Directly, my new young friend became a committed believer, began Christian schooling, and before long was pastoring a church. After many years, I learned that he was a settled and respected pastor.

I had long forgotten a probing comment I once made, but it came to light in a conversation following a church service I attended. While talking with a young man who was about to be launched into missionary service, I was sharing with him the importance of distinguishing between the promptings of the Spirit and simple emotional enthusiasm. "Look for definite guidance from the Holy Spirit," I urged. Just then his father and mother approached us and joined in the conversation.

"Do you remember what you said to me many years ago when we first met, back when I was a single guy?" asked the young man's father. "I asked you about my possible involvement with a lady in the church who had three children from a previous relationship. After a brief pause, this is what you said, and it changed my life: 'The further you want to go in serving God, the more God will expect from you in dedication.' That searching statement changed my life! Now here I am with the wife God had for me. This son standing here about to become a missionary would not even exist if you had not answered me in the way you did!"

Chapter 15

A Hand of Rescue to Fallen Leaders

No one in our church would have dreamed that Bill and Kim, popular missionaries to a distant land, were mired in their own spiritual life-or-death struggle. I met them for the first time when they returned with their children for some months on home assignment. Reluctantly, she came for a visit at my office. (I believe this came about because her husband was being stirred in his heart at our weekly men's meetings, and I encouraged him to have her also talk with me.) The encounter proved to be a testy one.

I soon came to realize that she was well experienced in professional counseling of all sorts, and I detected a strong odor of disdain for the efforts of her own pastor. Her guard was up, and the moment I started to open my Bible, she said, "And don't read that to me—I've heard all that over all the years of my hurt!"

I responded by slowly closing the Bible and placing it symbolically in the center of my desk. "I know you are in much distress, and this hurts me also. You and Bill are much loved by our church. What makes me doubly sad is that I know something that would truly help you, and yet you do not allow me to share it."

"What could you possibly know that I have not already heard over and again as I've struggled to get out of this unhappy state?"

Praying a desperate prayer in the secret of my heart, I continued, "Kim, I care very much for you and Bill. Please let me help. I have a plan of release for you."

"All right," she said with an air of challenge, "I'm listening, tell me."

"But you won't allow me because my plan requires me to open the Bible"—here I pointed to the closed Scripture.

"Go ahead, then," she said quietly. Realizing that I was working against years of inner scar tissue layered there by abortive counsel from doctors and psychologists and some pastors, I prayed aloud briefly for God's special assistance. Then I opened to Hebrews and read verses on Christ's offering of his blood on Calvary's altar. She listened quietly as I stressed that, when one claims this sacrifice as one's very own, God completely forgives all sin against him. Then he is free to give exactly the help that we most need. (And I knew her needs were very deep and indeed painful. My heart ached for her because of the years of suffering she had endured.)

Soon after sharing these thoughts with her, she left for home, having agreed to a possible future meeting with me. I knew this next session would be crucial, so I gained her permission to have a faithful elder sit with us. It proved to be a remarkable encounter between God and his wandering, struggling child. In the light of more Scripture and earnest prayer, I led her to see that her husband was not really the cause of her woes, which traced back to her earliest memories.

Suddenly she sat straight up in her chair, with tears brimming from her widened eyes, and gasped, "What! You mean all these years of suffering—and I'm the one? *I* caused all this?"

"Yes, the ultimate blame is yours. But it is also true that 'the blood of Jesus, his Son, purifies us from all sin' (1 John 1:7)." At my suggestion, Kim slipped to her knees and, with a flood of tears, made a full confession of her lifetime of rebellion, which had led to so much confusion.

The following Sunday she stood at the pulpit beside her husband and, facing the congregation who had supported them as missionaries over many years, spoke these words. "For years while you supported us as your missionaries, I lived in hatred of the man standing beside me. I have confessed my sin to God and to my family, and now I must make things right with you." As can be imagined, her tears were greeted with shock and the congregation's own tears.

Along with further counsel and other support, I paid a visit to the home and talked together with Bill and Kim and their two children. The atmosphere was clear and relaxed. I ended the session by having us all kneel in prayer, and everyone offered his or her own moving prayer of thanksgiving and request for further help from God.

Chapter 16

Helping the Unwilling to Be Willing

Hearing about the new lady's "godless and impossible" husband stirred within me a desire to talk personally with him. When I visited the home, I found him in the back yard with garden hose in hand, watering his plants. As soon as I introduced myself, he turned back to his watering without any word of acknowledgment. I continued our one-sided conversation until I was sure of his true feelings. Not wishing to cheapen my message, I said frankly, "You seem not to be pleased with my visit. Would you like me to leave now?"

"Yes, that's right." He spoke these words with scarcely a side glance at me and continued watering his garden.

"OK, Greg, if that's your choice, I'll leave now and not return until you choose to call for me." With that, I turned and left the home. A few weeks later he called for my help to restore his broken marriage and spare his children from the misery they were enduring.

He agreed to meet weekly with me, and I soon saw the pitiful heart and life behind his hard facade. All his life he had hidden his inferior feelings at being unable to read, even at a first-grade level. Though he was amazingly deft at getting his associates at work to read any form he had to sign, he was totally unable to handle his own inferior complex.

Slowly, he let me into his secret prison as we began meeting weekly to read through a gospel, bit by bit, I gradually got him to attempt audible reading, complimenting him for each new step of progress. The first time, I burst forth with, "You see, Greg, you can read! All you need is more practice and less worrying about it. God will help us right here to learn." And learn he did, as we read through several Bible books, taking turns. We both were blessed in this fellowship.

His bouts of drunkenness that so threatened the peace of his home stopped at once, and when I moved away shortly afterward, it was with gratitude to God for progress made.

Several years later, however, I was sad to learn that he had fallen again into his addictions. While in town, I went to the hospital and found him with serious throat cancer. With glad surprise and great shame, he looked into my face and attempted to speak. This was no time for niceties. "You have fallen back into sin, haven't you, Greg?"

"Yes," he nodded with an affirmative sound through the opening in his throat. He was a sad sight indeed, but he readily surrendered and got back on track with God and his wife. So far as I know, he died in peace.

Thoughtfully I read and commented on the Ten Commandments to a very intelligent and scholarly-type couple. Len was finishing another advanced degree at the university, where a cleaning lady had pressed him and his wife to have an appointment with me. We were seated at my kitchen table when I applied the just-read Scripture to their personal lives and inquired pointedly (with prayer in my heart), "Len and Sue, have you broken any of these laws of God?" I knew they were filled with academic doubts and questions about the Christian faith.

That is why I chose to start the interview like I did, hoping to pierce their consciences.

Exactly that happened when Sue exclaimed, "All, Len, all—we've broken them all!" Len tucked his head with a sheepish grin of agreement. There, at my kitchen table, we bowed, and God seemed to be present with his forgiving grace.

My visit to an unchurched man in the hospital seemed to be welcomed, but he was a rough one, constantly cursing! So I read him the Ten Commandments, taking time to apply them to his life.

"Have you broken God's laws?" I asked.

"No, I try not to do wrong things."

"But I just heard you break this very command: 'You shall not misuse the name of the LORD your God, for the LORD will not hold anyone guiltless who misuses his name'" (Exod. 20:7). I recall that, after this interaction, he was quite receptive to my further words.

Chapter 17

Raising Cloudy Curtains and Bringing Light

The minister's meeting erupted and fell apart, but the real problem was that it was in our home! It was our turn to host this monthly gathering. As soon as the last one exited our front door, my wife turned toward me with hands on her hips and said, "Why on earth did you do that?!" My answer did not help.

What I did was to liven the evening meeting with a riddle: Suppose a man comes to your study door, upset and discouraged. He is a professing Christian and member of your church who has fallen back into his former sin of drunkenness. What do you say to him?

As I expected, my brothers answered by saying they would pray with him, using 1 John 1:9, and then send him out with the help of 1 Corinthians 10:13.

I continued the riddle: "Days later he is back again at your door, very discouraged. Now what do you do to help him?" The brethren agreed that 1 John 1:9 and 1 Corinthians 10:13 were still their tools of choice.

"This continues to happen over and again—now what?" At that point, things fell apart, and I could not manage to get all the loose feathers back into the pillow.

My convictions about this matter have not changed. While it is true that one with an addiction must confess and name the sin, he or she needs to go further than simply hand the right label to God, along with a prayer for forgiveness. Rather, such a person must renounce and repent of the sin. In this holy transaction the guilty person must clearly embrace (1) Christ's cross as the awful, required punishment for this very sin and (2) the resurrection power of the Lord, brought to him by the Holy Spirit.

Convincing attorneys to listen to Scripture was a big challenge, but it happened. A businessman I had discipled persuaded a strong, high-profile trial lawyer to meet with us for lunch. Little did we know what this would lead to! (And none of this would have happened if I had not taken time to teach my friend in weekly sessions, using my plan of discipling as taught in my *Spiritual Life Studies* manual).

It was obvious that the attorney was used to coming to a point with words, so I applied the Gospel straight to his heart and life. With a kind of bluntness, he responded, "Tell me, then, what do you want me to do about this?"

I said flatly, "I want you to go with me to my car right now, bow your head, and in your own words tell God that you have broken his laws by sinning against him and that you now believe in the Lord Jesus Christ as your Savior." Without hesitation, he stood straight to his feet and said decisively, "Let's do it!"

In the car we each prayed. His prayer was both simple and moving. I then challenged him to devise a way to gather his legal colleagues for Bible study. He was an influential man, and several prominent lawyers from the city's political and legal community agreed to join him. Thus began an interesting chapter as the church's influence was extended in new directions.

The men readily agreed to meet in the church's board room. The first couple of meetings were, as the street expression goes, knock-down, drag-out affairs. Each new controversial item I brought up was assailed from both sides of the table, although they generally were more after each another than against me.

I knew my time would come, and it did. As a group, they agreed that they would like me to review for them the state's canons of law regarding morality and ethics, which served to guide all their practice. This was great! Now I could cover many Bible truths about righteous living and repeatedly draw them to the cross for forgiveness. I found them more keenly aware of right and wrong than I had expected.

"I often can argue an opposition party around in circles until they are so unnerved that they agree with what they know is not true, but I excuse this in my mind because I have a contractual obligation to defend my client and win his case. Where is the line between right and wrong in all this?" Many such questions had to be faced.

However, the big showdown came in our study of these canons of ethics when I tackled the ruling that requires lawyers to counsel their clients not to defend themselves but rather to rely on an attorney to be their advocate. A full section on the dire consequences of self-advocacy was right there in this legal document. This provided me with a very special opportunity.

All the attorneys gave their intense attention as I made my point. "Gentlemen, we all agree that having to advocate one's own cause can be a disaster. But when the time comes for you to face the greatest tribunal of all—and it is appointed unto all of us to die and to face our God—are you going to fall back on self-advocacy? Where is your advocate then? What is his name?" At this rather dramatic moment, I read to them these words of Scripture:

> But if anybody does sin, we have one who speaks to
> the Father in our defense—Jesus Christ, the Righteous
> One. He is the atoning sacrifice for our sins, and not
> only for ours but also for the sins of the whole world.
> (1 John 2:1-2)

This setting provided an excellent opportunity to explain the riches of propitiation and then of Christ's representation of us before the Father.

Another opportunity presented itself to use this same approach when I became friends with a professional advocate for the five or six hundred physicians in our city. We became acquainted when I was injured as a patient in the hospital by an aide's mistake during therapy. Though the injury was significant and the hospital admitted fault, I told them that I would not be suing but simply wanted them to care for all the expenses I incurred while healing from the injury caused by their improper care.

My new friend volunteered to be my advocate and make sure that the hospital covered their portion of my expenses. Here was my opportunity.

Seated one morning in the hospital coffee shop, I said to him, "You have been kind to me, and I deeply appreciate how you have been my advocate over and again. Now I must tell you that, when you appear before the Lord God in the day of judgment, you must have an advocate. The only one worthy and able to win your case is the Lord Jesus Christ." Then and there he willingly bowed his head and prayed aloud. As staff persons known to him walked by, he humbly asked Christ for salvation and right standing before God.

The host pastor invited his Sunday morning congregation to ask questions of me in a public session. God's Spirit seemed to be working openly and deeply in our midst. One lady asked a typical question that I answered, but I felt there was more behind her agitated spirit than she was saying. So I gently inquired how other matters were in her life. Readily and openly she confessed lifelong bitterness toward her parents. The following conversation ensued, with me standing at the right front of the church. She was on the opposite side near the front but speaking loudly enough for everyone to hear.

"I can tell you now," I said, "on the basis of what you just said, you are a person who struggles against fear, worry, and apprehension over impending things—are you not?"

"Oh, yes!" she said, with a kind of gasp, "but how did you know?"

"From the Bible. First John 4:18 says, 'There is no fear in love. But perfect love drives out fear.' Since perfect love is the required antidote for fear, if your love is flawed by any bitterness or hatred, fear creeps in. Where light is not, the dark is."

This exchange seemed to touch not only her but the congregation as well.

Being converted by a wrong spirit—that was the only explanation possible for Jean's experience. She had grown up in our church but had somehow gotten emotionally involved with a married man from another faith who was ten or fifteen years her senior. Now she was taking instructions in his religion.

By her mother's intervention, she agreed to meet with me. Her first words were, "Oh, Pastor, I know that I have truly found the Lord and been born anew!" Her face shone in agreement with her words. Nothing I said managed to unseat what appeared to me to be a false confidence.

In an effort to at least stop her immoral involvement and create breathing room for further counsel, I read her John 10:27-28, "My sheep listen to my voice; I know them, and they follow me. I give them eternal life."

Then I asked her, "Is Jesus Christ your Savior and Shepherd?"

"Oh, yes, I've never been so sure of that as now."

"Then you will surely obey the voice of your shepherd according to his own words here in this text. Notice also that the ones to whom he gives eternal life are the ones who obey and follow his voice. He clearly forbids the type of relationship you are considering. Will you now turn from that and follow the voice of your Shepherd? You *must* if you are his."

Still clinging to her false notions, she left my office. Later I told her mother that Jean had undoubtedly had a definite "conversion" experience—but by the wrong spirit.

A "dishpan vision" was claimed by a young woman who often attended our evening services. Briefly, her story is this: she had become enamored with a young pastor. Realizing the jeopardy of this situation, I arranged for her to meet with my wife and me in our home one evening following the service.

That was when I learned that she had had some kind of "vision" while doing dishes and felt the Lord had appeared to her and had given his sanction and encouragement to this lustful dream of hers. Here again I used with considerable spiritual force John 10:27-28, much in the same manner as in the story just told. As I recall, she was at least stopped from this sinful dream.

Something was terribly wrong with Grace. She and her husband were both educators and openly confessed Christ as they prepared to join our fellowship. She had some emotional struggles that continued to cloud her life and made it difficult for her responsibilities as a mother to three younger children.

The depth of her difficulty was shown to me one Sunday after the service when she came to me and asked pitifully, "Pastor, could you please show me the door. I want to get to my family waiting in the car." It dawned on me that she was so "lost" that she really was unaware of the numerous exits all around. I took her out to the parking lot and to her waiting family.

"We'd better talk at once—phone me," I whispered to the husband. His call filled out the picture for me. It was indeed a crisis. For more than ten years, Grace had received professional psychological help of all kinds, but yet she grew steadily worse. We agreed that something new—totally different—had to be done, and done at once. She was breaking down. The completely new departure agreed on was one that I have not often recommended: "Flush all her medications down the toilet, and bring her to the church for immediate counsel and prayer!" He greeted this idea with considerable enthusiasm. And so, an hour or so before the evening service, she came to my study at the church. It was a very special meeting as we sought our Lord's face in prayer together and asked for an intervention of the Holy Spirit. (Looking back over many years, let me assure the reader that God answered our desperate plea.)

Before our session ended and we went to the church service, I said to Grace, "You haven't had any supper, have you?"

"No," she replied, "but I'll be OK." At this, I produced my peanut butter and jelly sandwich from home, which I shared with her. We sat together and thanked God for all his provisions. It was a veritable Communion service! God was healing her and blessing me.

All was not easy, however. There were spiritual strongholds of long standing and very deep roots in her life. Once, as these roots were being exposed and we were bowed in prayer, she began to curse me in a most awful way, using a strange voice and manifesting a very hostile attitude. No one would have thought her capable of such a thing! But we persisted, and her deliverance was sure and complete.

Later, for several years, I taught a course on biblical counseling at a Christian graduate school. I regularly called on students to lean on Scripture in their counseling, but not too heavily on medicinal therapy. In one such class, a nursing professional pointedly resisted this approach. It so happened that Grace herself was there in the classroom that very day, for she had traveled to the school to attend my course. Raising her hand, she asked meekly, "Pastor, may I come and tell my story?"

I welcomed her to the podium and the mike. She presented herself to the students as an example of one who had tried the best of professional help for well over a decade but was left teetering on a complete breakdown. Then she told what had happened in her life and pled with the students to listen carefully to the teaching that had saved her life and spared her family great harm.

Back at her home church, she developed a counseling ministry among women, with obvious blessing from God.

Chapter 18

All Spiritual War Is Tough and Might Involve Demons

Hiding from encounters with evil spirits is not possible if one gets into the thick of the battle. However, the apostle Paul is shown on one occasion (Acts 16:16-18) avoiding the exorcism as long as he could. But whenever such a showdown was called for, he proceeded victoriously.

The most experienced spiritual warrior and "demon chaser" I ever knew fell into immorality himself with one he was attempting to help. (May I never forget this warning!) Dealing with deeper darkness can be dangerous if one is not shielded by the Lord Jesus Christ. Several times my life has been threatened.

Unexpectedly, Joe, a close friend and Christian worker with whom I had much contact, began to show a strange side. Whatever his problem was, it surfaced one day as I was questioning him about his background. Suffice it to say that he had had a violent youth. As I questioned him, seated at my table at home with my wife present, he became angry, stood up to his more than six feet, and rained down threatening words on me. I knew his threats were not idle. Just then, my wife interrupted and spoke with great authority, "Oh, sit down, Joe! No one is intimidated by you!" And down he dropped into his chair. He confided to me later, "I am not afraid of anybody except your wife. I am terrified by her." The spirit in him knew the Spirit in my wife.

On another occasion, I took a missionary from Africa along with me to visit Joe. My practice was to give varied training experiences to our missionaries while they were on home assignment. Seated in Joe's front room, things became tense at once. As we sought God's face in prayer, he became very agitated and even threatening.

"Get out of here, Harold, while you can. I'm going to kill you!" I saw a pistol-sized bulge in his right trouser pocket and knew very well that I would not be the first human target in his personal history.

Of course, this was a shaking experience, but it seemed very wrong to head for the door in the face of such a challenge. Instead, I stood and walked slowly toward him saying, "No, you're not going to do anything, Joe. I bind you, evil spirit, in the name of the Lord Jesus Christ." At this, he roared threateningly, "If you untie my hands, I will kill you." He began jerking his arms up from the arms of the chair, but they seemed invisibly tied, and he sat back, unable to mount any assault. When he was quieted, I prayed for the deliverance of my friend, but with uncertain effect.

My missionary friend and I soon left and on the way home reviewed the evening's events. I explained that his assigned field abroad would surely bring such encounters as we had just experienced. He admitted that his limbs were shaking throughout the evening—as were mine, much of the time. Considerable light was thrown on the depths of this poor man's bondage to evil spirits when I later learned from him that he had made some kind of blood covenant with Satan.

One other encounter with this man occurred when he showed up at church one Sunday morning and spoke threateningly to my wife as to what he was about to do to me. She sent me an urgent message of warning, but the service was about to begin. I told my associate who would be sitting beside me on the platform, "If anyone uninvited attempts to enter the pulpit area, perhaps through these curtains behind our chairs, I want you immediately to throw him to the floor and pin him there. A man is threatening to kill me." It was comforting that my associate was young and muscular. Not very long after this, the man moved away, and I also moved to another assignment.

A young mother and her two very young children stood at my door completely soaked in the pouring rain. Jane and I welcomed them to our fireside, where we heard the sad story of abuse by her husband, Jim, who had literally driven them out into the rain with no protection. More than that, a demonic presence seemed to hover about the man. I sensed the evil, unmistakably.

I had recently met Jim and counseled at least once with him. Directly after that meeting, a psychologist contacted me with the distressing news that I was dealing with a dangerous man. He was indeed paranoid, even to the point of stretching very thin lines of string across his driveway at home so he could tell if any other man had visited his wife while he was at work. She was a gentle, sincere believer, still attempting to keep the family together, but he was a restless soul. Furthermore, a violent side to his character began to emerge. He came to my home one day with a loaded .45 automatic, which he handed over to me; for a while, I kept it from him in my study file.

On another occasion his wife called me, warning me that Jim was headed to my home and had the gun in his possession. I was forced to hide my wife and kids in an upstairs room. I instructed them to pile all the furniture against the door while I awaited his coming. He never came; in fact, the police finally arrested him and allowed him to go free only with the stipulation that he was not to go near his wife.

Finally (picking up the story from her appearance at our front door), Jim's wife packed her belongings and the children's things and headed for the train station, purchasing tickets back to her home in the South. While she and I were standing outside the station, talking and waiting for the train, Jim suddenly appeared to plead with her, and she began a loud wailing cry, "No, no, I can't take anymore!" (I had made definite arrangements with the police that they ought to have armed guards at the station to prevent this very thing from happening, but they were late in arriving!) Confronting Jim, I strongly ordered him to leave, telling him that the police were coming and would not allow this kind of contact. He turned and fled into the distant shadows. She continued to weep and sob hysterically, "He'll be back, he'll be back—I know him."

Then she suddenly cried out in a loud wail, "Oh, he took my money, he picked my purse!" Now she could not pay for their tickets. The train was just approaching. Searching my wallet, I found some folded money in a side pocket and pressed that in her hand and gained permission to board her, explaining that she could pay her way at least to New York. The police had finally arrived, but she was still crying, "But he will be on board. I know that he will slip aboard and get us!" I quickly made two promises to quiet her. "I will have the police right now search the entire train. And then I will call New York police to have them meet you and board you safely on the final leg of your journey. All will be well." We prayed and she left.

I phoned the New York police and informed them of the full story. Then I phoned her parents and urged them to wire money to the station. In any event, she had no further interruptions. Eventually she made it home safely with her children and fell exhausted into the arms of her waiting family.

Let me emphasize again that, regarding demons or evil spirits, two extremes must be avoided: to be forever *looking over* demons, seeing them everywhere, or else to be *overlooking* them. Sometimes it seems impossible to stay on higher solid ground and at the same time stay in the battle.

More than once I have witnessed collapsed victims, down on all fours, drooling mucus and saliva, or even vomiting a green substance. Or episodes like a possessed young woman fighting hand to hand with several police officers who were attempting unsuccessfully to subdue her.

Another time I went to see a dying woman who had for years practiced as a spirit medium. She was a gruesome sight; only a skeleton remained. Before I could say a word, the skeleton's eyes opened, and with a hissing sound she raised herself in bed and issued this curse on me, "I wish you were in hell!" And then more hissing.

Chapter 19

The Power of Words
Spoken in Love

A scene that will always be precious to me occurred one day in my office between a young man and a young woman, Miriam, engaged to be married. It was preceded, however, by a visit from Miriam, who entered and seated herself in obvious distress. There was something deep in her heart that had to come out. Recently engaged, she wanted so badly to make everything right in her life with God.

Out came the admission amid many tears and wrenching sobs. She had been at one time involved in immorality and felt she ought to make this known and open to her future husband. I suggested that she bring him to the office and let me help. She agreed.

After prayer with the two of them, I said to the young man, "Miriam has something she wants to tell you." Then, shaking with tears, she poured out her confession, staring straight ahead.

A dramatic pause followed as this future husband slowly turned toward Miriam and said only four words with an earnest emphasis, "Miriam, I love you!" With that, she fell into his arms and they wept together. All was well.

Another incident demonstrates God's blessing on the pastor who leaves the platform and goes into the homes. Henry was a man who drank heavily and never set foot in the church. His wife came regularly to our church but was much ashamed of her husband and preferred that he stayed closeted at home. Much to her chagrin, I stopped by their home when she was out so I could visit Henry.

I sensed that he was a bit numbed by alcohol, yet he seemed open and receptive to the truths that I pressed upon his heart. So I made a second visit and found him even more responsive. In fact, I loved this ruffled fellow, and he was obviously warming toward me. As I stood to leave, it seemed wrong to let him still be dangling in his spiritual indecision.

Facing him, I grabbed each of his arms and, looking him squarely in the eyes, said, "Man, I'm going to heaven, but I don't want to go without you. I care about you. You must call upon the Lord Jesus just as I have explained." And he did—standing right there in the middle of the room.

My next challenge was to quiet Henry's agitated wife and help her see that the condition of her husband's soul was much more important than anything that might have been out of place when I entered their home. "Henry needs me because he needs the Lord Jesus Christ." Quietly she agreed. Next Sunday, there he was, sitting beside her in church. Poor man! He was wearing the only suit he had, brought out from some long-unused closet. But it was thick wool, not the best choice for a blazing-hot day in midsummer! Henry was sweating profusely.

Finally, our schedule included an outing together. Henry confided that he used to go to a certain favorite restaurant in his younger, sober days—and he would like to visit there again, if I cared to go with him. What a time we had! He was a perfect host, alert, sensitive, and quite at ease. I felt like I was witnessing a friend emerging from years in prison and rejoining society. After lunch, we headed home but stopped along the way at a favorite spot he used to visit by the lake. Our fellowship and conversation were just what you'd expect of two believers.

A litany of sins, problems, and heartache could be detailed about another couple, but God had brought them through every crisis, and they were determined to have God perfect what he had begun in their lives. Therefore, the three of us agreed on a plan. John and Fran would go away on their own spiritual retreat, spending the total time praying and meditating on an assigned Scripture.

My assigned text was the book of 1 John, from beginning to end. They needed to clear the channels between themselves and also with God. Their problems were real and deep, but God's Word worked powerfully. Their day-and-night praying brought insights they had never sensed before. Their love was greatly enhanced. The plan worked because, simply put, God wants us to be right even more than we want it. He is not hiding. He is available with all his power and glory. His Word, when received deeply, has power that is beyond earthly bounds. Amen!

Conclusions

What I Have Learned about God through His Dealings with Me

I wish here and now to confess and emphasize that my advanced age and years of service are no explanation for any special works of God I have here recorded. The power in an electrical line is not determined by its years in service but by the Power Source.

Even the preaching and counseling words came from God's Spirit as inner promptings. Many times, not knowing exactly what to say or to do next, I might interrupt an interview, saying, "Let's pray again." Sometimes my prayer was more of a laboring or a struggling. At other times needed insights came as a quiet prompting in answer to a quick, silent prayer.

It also must be added that things that seem more spectacular when told, seemed more ordinary as they were experienced. At the time, they only seemed to be natural and simply "right." Or putting it another way, those happenings seemed like what "ought to be," assuming my partnership was truly with God.

In addition, God protects his weak children by causing special answers to prayer to seem more ordinary to the one who is praying. An over-confident, proud, bouncy attitude is obnoxious to our God.

God's eye is on the little ones, the weak ones, not the strong movers and shakers. A lethal but prevalent disease among

Christian leaders is what I call "big stuffism." Too many preachers and Christian workers want to appear big. But this attitude leaves our churches not knowing how to use and deploy the little ones in the church. By "little," of course, I mean, those who are less prominent, more retiring, poorer in material means, or plain in their way of thinking and speaking. None of these descriptions tells us one whit of what God may have for these specially valued members of Christ's body in the way of spiritual gifts—if only they were properly and patiently discipled.

Directions toward New Life; or, How to Get There from Here

Stay everlastingly in prayer.

- extended prayer each morning (preparing each night for the next morning's prayer by a disciplined guarding against late-night TV and the like);
- throughout every day;
- special, planned seasons of prayer, sometimes supported by at least brief fasting and withdrawal from the regular schedule.

Stay everlastingly at edification.

- regular discipling of individuals (Except for special ongoing efforts at reproducing other leaders, keep these personal sessions on schedule in terms of time spent and the number of meetings held; aim at discipling those who disciple others.);
- spontaneous efforts to encourage, upbuild, or warn in all daily contacts; put shots of truth into lives all day long, every day.

Do not spend time in self-promotion; be more than you tell.

Refuse and resist Satan—definitely, using Scripture.

Receive and use each trial for your own benefit.

> Remember that fruit from deep trials does not come immediately. Invariably there is a gestation period. Our impatient natures incline to strip the fruit prematurely from the womb, not trusting that God will, in his own time, bring things to light just as he promises:

> > How great is your goodness,
> > > which you have stored up for those
> > > > who fear you,
> > which you bestow in the sight of men
> > > on those who take refuge in you.
> > > > (Ps. 31:19)

Final Words and Testimony

1. Watch out for those who feel they are *too busy*. This feeling of being weary in well doing is a veritable "common cold" among church leaders. Back in World War II, I coined this saying in mild sarcasm: "Each of you feels he's the busiest man on earth. You're all wrong—I am!"

2. Again, this common cold is apt to linger long, and it is highly contagious. Irritability and a tired drag can be passed along.

3. Do not put yourself "up for grabs" as to schedule, phone interruptions, or visitors. Prepare ahead of time with God in prayer and Bible reading as to how and where you will spend your day.

4. Distinguish between Bible study (where you are seeking God's message for others) and your own time with God and

Scripture (when you are seeking to hear personally from God).

5. God will repeatedly rein in with testings those to whom he wants to display himself. This will involve a stripping process in which God wars against our sinful attitudes, actions, ambitions, and finally even some things we had supposed to be our "strengths"—that our reliance will be totally on him. Sooner or later we must learn the depths of the apostle's meaning in Philippians 3:8-11:

> What is more, I consider everything a loss compared to the surpassing greatness of knowing Christ Jesus my Lord, for whose sake I have lost all things. I consider them rubbish, that I may gain Christ and be found in him, not having a righteousness of my own that comes from the law, but that which is through faith in Christ—the righteousness that comes from God and is by faith. I want to know Christ and the power of his resurrection and the fellowship of sharing in his sufferings, becoming like him in his death, and so, somehow, to attain to the resurrection from the dead.

6. I have always thought of myself as warring, always in a battle and destined one day to make a final strike and topple across heaven's threshold. Also, I must confess to an ever-present feeling of being not "at home" any place in this world. Always it seems there is some other place I am yet to come to.

7. Life is made up of an unending series of contests, or wars, if you will. Our duty is to make the next due surrender to the Lord. When Jesus stood face to face with the devil, the

enemy promised, "Yield, and I will give you very much." In remarkable contrast, Jesus still says to us, "Take up your cross and follow me. If you want to gain, you must lose."

8. Be sure you know more, and experience more, than you tell.

9. A pastor does not know as much as he needs to know until he is able to train others to do what he does. Elders must be able to train others to be elders. The aim is to see that each one in the church is discipled and that all who can, will join in this disciple-making ministry. If this is done, the local church can train its own people to do works among children, young people, and men and women.

10. Keep ever in mind how Jesus and John the Baptist often pulled away from crowds to lonely places. In sad contrast, we today employ all sorts of means of public relations to get up a crowd. What is missing is not crowds but the Holy Spirit and his power.

11. Sometimes God's deeper works are hidden for a time and might be overlooked in discouragement. Often more grace is required to recognize God's work than is required to be the means he uses to accomplish that work.

12. Avoid the fatal euphoria mentioned in the text below:

> The seventy-two returned with joy and said, "Lord, even the demons submit to us in your name."
>
> He replied, "I saw Satan fall like lightning from heaven. I have given you authority to trample on snakes and scorpions and to overcome all the power of the enemy; nothing will harm you. However, do not rejoice that the spirits submit to you, but rejoice that your names are written in heaven." (Luke 10:17-20)

The only safe way to battle demons and do heroics is to keep your head down while facing enemy fire.

13. Keep well hidden from the applause of your friends. I think the devil fills the bleachers that surround us with a cheering section as well as a jeering section. Sometimes it is more dangerous to be adored by saints than to be hated by demons. One thing that provides a safe insulation against the risings of pride is humiliation that comes through suffering—unless you are an unusual saint and well disciplined in prayer and Scripture meditation.

14. Not all hard work is a "suffering for Jesus." Much Christian service is just plain hard work. That is, we must not let self-pity drive us to overdramatize things.

15. There's no way to suffer for Jesus without it hurting. I have discovered that the Heavenly Carpenter cuts every board he takes from the lumber stack for his building purposes. The only way to avoid the cutting is to stay stacked.

16. As true progress is made in our spiritual lives, an ordered peace should replace former confusion and disorder. Notice how Philippians 4:7 describes this condition: "And the peace of God, which transcends all understanding, will guard your hearts and your minds in Christ Jesus."

As we near the end of this writing, permit me to quote in full my extended personal testimony as I once gave it to missionary friends abroad. These lines were written many years ago, but they show the very paths down which God has directed me.

> I want to give you a testimony of God's work in my own life. With the passing of time, things have changed with me. My goals in "church work" are

different; my methodology (or program ideas) have greatly altered. By his grace, I myself am not what I was. As servants of Christ, we cannot escape it: God never calls us to "fill" a position, in the way we think of "filling the pulpit," or the like. "For this is the will of God, even your sanctification. . . . For God hath . . . called us . . . unto holiness" (1 Thess. 4:3, 7 KJV). Our *first* concern MUST be to BE what he wants; and once we get on with that, it turns out to be oh so different from what we expected!

Next, I am seeking to lead others along this same track. I am not THE minister. We are together servants of Christ, members of this one local body. Who knows what good "gift" will be bestowed? Where are there biblical elders and ministers, in the New Testament sense, *produced* by the church? My feeling is that a church can do far more than run a program, operate a budget, and then hire a professional "minister" to do its "ministering." What folly that we expect *you* [missionaries] to produce an indigenous church in that culture, from scratch, and we look to the seminaries and our all-sufficient budgets and thus "import" our "staff."

What a giant is the local assembly when filled by the Spirit! I feel like one commissioned to massage the sleeping members into a vital experience. This new life means a new love. I discover more homes are being opened as hearts are opened. Christians need each other. Preachers do not have all the gifts. We must cry to God to bring us up to the young church in Rome. They were "full of goodness, filled with all knowledge, able also to admonish one another" (Rom. 15:14 KJV)

The typical minister's life of pushing a rat-race schedule of programming and then toppling into a grave 'neath trees with abundant foliage and little fruit—this scares me. The years are already slipping by, so I want the Lord's help, and your prayers, as I get on with this boot camp. (Swatting flies far behind the battle lines makes good references for the next larger church but does not disturb the Enemy!)

What it would mean if we could present Christ with a new "body" here—into which new converts could be saved! There would be no more of that strolling "forward" to lightly "accept Jesus." The man who gets hold of a wire that is charged will pulsate with it. Frankly, I have begun to suspect that any good salesman could contact folks enough to fill up the empty seats, and maybe even get up his quota of "decisions." But a church full of "decided" folks who hold the same Bible views and make the same choices of public entertainment *is still not a church.*

Besides these things, here is a summary list of important attitudes that have been growing lately within my heart, and I trust within others:

1. The sinfulness of sin.
2. The sufficiency of Christ and what it means to be "in" our Head. (Rom. 6–8; 1 Cor. 1:30; Ephesians)
3. Absolute necessity for personal holiness. To continue practicing sin and profess Christ is impossible. Breaking with sin is a must. Philippians 1:6 does not say that we will be

saved *anyhow*. It says that those who are surely and securely God's children will be led on toward perfection. The others are none of his; there is no exception.

4. Growing hunger for God.

5. Love and concern for one another.

6. New regard for Satan, who powerfully thwarts us on every hand, unless the armor be complete and prayer constant.

7. Like babies learning to talk, we are now trying to pray—really pray—and faith appears like a first evening star: not too clear as yet, but with good prospects.

8. Some of our Savior's compassion for the multitudes of sheep without a shepherd.

It has taken too many years to get this little way. Jane and I are therefore asking God to help us teach our children all this. They need to know that there is no other *Christian* life except that which gets on with the matter of holiness and abandonment to God. A life that *intends* to be less than perfect is that of a rebel, not a son. (Incidentally, I no longer give the old invitation: "How many of you Christian young people would be willing to do this or that if the Lord should call you." The first thing is repentance—or perish [Luke 13:3], and one who has truly repented will not willingly resist his will [Heb. 10:26].) A new convert does not have much light, but he is responsible to submit to that which he has and be just as perfect as

God has called him to be. By our faulty preaching of repentance, faith, and security, we have oiled the tracks of backsliding and cushioned the place of sin. We need to help folks raise their guard against the flesh, Satan, and the world—deadly enemies.

My heart is full, and may the Holy Spirit minister abundantly to you as well.

Harold E. Burchett

Appendix

Humor Brightens the Way

Even little lights are bright when the tunnel is very dark. Humor also provides release from tension and heaviness.

To prevent my going to extremes or overindulging in any improper, distasteful "fun," I have long been aware of a deep, hidden faculty that I call my editorial committee. Theirs is a twenty-four-hour, seven-day-a-week responsibility that involves filling wastebaskets of ideas that are being edited out. I say twenty-four-hour task because it is not uncommon for me to stumble onto something humorous in the night or predawn hours.

An example of one item that finally passed committee after some reluctance on their part was the day I relocated my lost bottle of mustard. Preparing meals for my ailing wife and me was often more than I could handle. That day, my portion of our so-called meal consisted of an overcooked, dry hamburger patty on toast. It needed mustard, but the sight of the condiment troubled me. It was very dark indeed—and also was past the expiration date.

So I dialed the 800 number, as advised on the label, and explained, "I have just located an over-age bottle of your mustard. My sandwich here needs it—but is it safe to eat?"

"What does it look like?"

"Not pitch black, but almost."

(long pause) "Just a moment. I'll get advice." *(long, long wait)* Finally, "We think it's safe."

"But, ma'am, now I have another problem. That took so long, and I was so hungry—I ate the whole thing as is. Now what?"

(silence) "Well, I . . . uh. . . ."

"Oh well, thank you anyhow!"

When the editorial committee is not listened to, trouble is ahead. One example: Jane and I were seated at a nice white-linen table in a Toronto restaurant. When I wiped my nose with my handkerchief and, as always, was busy refolding it, Jane interrupted me, "Honey, please fold that under the table. Not in front of everyone." So I slid myself under the table, as ordered, and there in privacy, I folded the handkerchief. Then I poked my head up from beneath the linen tablecloth and asked,

"Did I do good?"

"Get up from there, Harold—you're making a scene!"

My intensity of focus causes me problems. One typical noontime, I dashed home from my church office for a quiet meal in our dining room with Jane. As usual, my schedule was filled with appointments awaiting my return. I made quick work of the meal and then was met with this embarrassing question. "Honey, how did you like the new recipe that I prepared?" Quickly I searched for any crumbs that might have escaped my last scoop from the plate. This futile effort was interrupted as my wife asked, "Do you even know what you ate?" The truth was, I had not the slightest idea. That dish was both good and gone.

The whole family shared in the fun of watching me go up and down the stairs at home, seeing how long it would take before I noticed that the door at the bottom of the stairs had been removed and was standing to one side. As unbelievable as it may seem, I even reached behind the misplaced door to get at the stairway light switch, without noticing that the door was where it shouldn't have been. Really, I desire to be focused—but not so unplugged!

I inherited kitchen duties on one occasion when Jane was called away to tend her mother for about three weeks. None of our children were nearby, so all household chores became my responsibility for the first time. In preparation for my initiation, Jane hung numerous notations and signs around the house. For example, I saw arrows pointing to the dryer and washer, with instructions, also notes on the refrigerator detailing all the preparations she had made and stocked within that appliance.

However, I still had to make decisions on my own. One morning when I was faced with preparing my breakfast, the thought occurred to me: rather than simply having scrambled eggs, why not put an additive in them? I recalled having seen bits of ham or the like mixed within scrambled eggs. Furthermore, I reasoned, if I cooked up an extra-large platter of this and ate it all at once, that would probably care for my noon meal also. After consuming that huge platter, sure enough, I wanted no more of anything that noon.

My next adventure came when I pulled out a TV dinner. Reading the directions carefully, I noticed that it didn't tell me to remove the contents from the box as a first step. Thus I reasoned that the container would be OK in the electric oven. First, however, I had to solve another problem—how to turn on the stove oven. Maybe it has lost power, I reasoned. But when I opened the oven door, the light came on, and when I closed the oven door, the light went off, indicating power was on hand. After a time of study, I figured out the sequence of settings and finally got things going up to temperature.

My next problem came when I knelt down and peered at my box inside and saw that it was turning brown. I was in danger of losing my directions, as the box was being baked, so I quickly grabbed pen and paper and copied them down so I would know when to extract my dinner. Studying my directions, I learned that the dinner was considered just right when it was a golden brown. Now my problem was this: I had all kinds of colors—like a rainbow—but the brown was just getting started. I reasoned, though, that enough was enough, so I shut things down and extracted the remains. Then I scraped off what was left of the original container, picking out as much of the lid as I could, and ate the meal.

I learned shortly afterward not to recount this experience in the wrong company. Even family and friends have reacted in utter disbelief and negative judgment toward one who could be so inept.

My appearance in court to face the judge came about because I drove by a police cruiser on my way to be the special speaker at a church's anniversary celebration. Just after I passed the police car, I made a right turn and then was abruptly stopped by the officer, who said I had gone through a stop sign. Since I was pressed for time, I didn't bother to argue my case. Later, however, I returned to the scene of the crime and found that the so-called stop sign was bent nearly double and was unreadable.

Some days later two police officers showed up on the steps of my church with a summons to appear in their town court. On the appointed day, I sat in the waiting room by the clerk's office. Soon he came out and asked, "Are you a church minister?"

"Yes."

"Why didn't you tell the officer?"

"He didn't ask me. And besides, if I did something wrong, what difference would that make? But in this case, I did nothing wrong. The traffic sign is not readable. Take a look for yourself."

"Well, we don't want a minister on our records." Later the clerk returned to where I was sitting and asked, "How are you going to plead?"

"If I'm asked whether I turned that corner without stopping, I will say that I did." Soon the court was convened. Out of all the crowd of sad looking characters present, my case was called first. I was urged to enter a plea of nolo contendere, and the arresting officer and I were called to approach the bench for a private word. (At this point I was beginning to feel sorry for all the mess and confusion I was causing the fine looking arresting officer, the clerk, and the judge.) After this short word with the judge, his gavel sounded and he intoned, "Case dismissed for want of prosecution."

While teaching in graduate school I was invited to be guest speaker in a church located in a nearby town. After my message, a lady almost disarmed me asking, "Are you sure you are a professor at the school?"

"Yes, I am."

"That's hard to believe. You sure don't talk like a professor. I understood every word you said."

Hoping this was a compliment, I managed this reply, "Well, ma'am, I guess that's because I don't know many big words." With that she seemed satisfied.

Another experience at the school showed that humor sometimes mingled with tears. As I was teaching and pointing out the wonderful privilege of being a pastor, tears would often well up in my eyes as I remembered how it once was with me. The president, a personal friend, heard of this and sent for me. Seated in front of his desk, he presented me with the question, "Harold, you are not happy teaching here, are you?"

Immediately I assured him that it was a great experience and honor for me to teach there with such quality colleagues. Then I added, "Yes, I really miss being a pastor, but which would you rather have teaching the students here—a happy little professor who has never done pastoral work himself, or one such as I who is aching to be back doing it himself?"

"OK, Burchett, I understand. Go ahead with your work!"

One of my admonitions to students was, Be ready for anything. For example, I casually answered the phone one night, only to be greeted by a lady's piercing screams, which continued one after another, desperate and loud.

"Who are you?" I demanded.

More screams. Then I heard a baby crying in the background. "Keep still and answer me. Who are you? What is your name?"

"No! No! Stop kicking him. You're killing him!" Screams. Baby's outcries grow louder.

I was desperate to do something to help—anything, but what? Where? Who?

Finally, I was able to gather a brief sketch of the mystery. A young couple had one infant child and a cat. The father was angry at something and kicked the cat, which woke and frightened the baby. This drove the hysteric mother to appeal to me, her pastor, for emergency rescue. But she forgot to give any and all essential information that I would need to help.

When I married Jane, she was a "proper Bostonian," so I felt the challenge to offer training in having fun. She allowed me to be chairman of the Family Entertainment Committee, but she insisted on my agreeing frequently to having a quiet mealtime. Our home also was a center for neighborhood action such as the display and sale of snakes and other vermin.

One highlight moment for my family was when I finally convinced Jane to put on boxing gloves with me. As a couple of neighbors watched in shocked amazement, I quickly learned what a bad idea this was. I competed on my knees, and she laid into me with both hands. I had no choice but to defend myself and to tap her once or twice on the nose. This was counterproductive, as she became very excited and began swinging from all directions, assaulting me with all her might.

Only two choices remained for me: either strike her or give up. I did the latter willingly. This event was a subject for laughter for many years.

Friends who visited us were often in for a treat—or a treatment! This might mean a raucous wake-up call as the family posted themselves up and down the stairs and let fly pots and pans. Or they might be treated to a large plastic spider under their table napkin—made to leap out when I yanked on the hidden string.

Another example of this victimization was when our future son-in-law was treated to his first meal in our home after his engagement to my daughter. My wife substituted a hard plastic hamburger in his supper sandwich. The poor fellow was at a great psychological disadvantage, so after he unsuccessfully bit it, he politely and unobtrusively turned it so as to make another attack on the trick burger. It wasn't long until all of my family burst out in laughter.

Returning missionaries who were close friends of mine provided choice opportunities for fun. As a former seminary classmate approached our front door, I gave him a warm greeting, only I called him by his father's name. With hand extended, I said, "It is so good to see you—but I was expecting Junior."

The poor fellow was completely derailed and stammered, "Well . . . you, uh . . . uh . . . I am 'Junior.' It's been a really hard term there in Pakistan." When he realized my mischief, we both laughed until tears came.

Another couple arriving from years away serving in the mountains of Tibet rang the doorbell. I was all prepared with my props. Jane's wheelchair was ready for me right at the front door, and as I positioned myself in it, I tossed a shawl around my shoulders and opened the door to greet them. He audibly gasped and stammered, "I thought . . . I didn't realize . . . what's wrong?"

"Nothing!" I cried enthusiastically, as I jumped to my feet. "Seeing you has made me feel great!"

Sometimes humor backfires, but I think I am a slow learner from this. A pastor and his wife, close friends of ours, had joined us for lunch in our home. Our dessert brownies were a bit hard to bite, so I made light of this by stabbing mine with my fork and pounding the handle with my double fist as if I were trying to pierce the square—but to no avail.

In mischief, I rolled my eyes toward my wife, who was not responding to the joke. I suddenly understood the dynamics when our guest pastor's wife said, "I made them." Somehow, mercy was shown to me, and the incident became our joke from then on.

Even with my wife's dealing with Alzheimer's Disease, we still had some fun together. Humor served at times to lighten the heavy load. I devote an entire chapter in my book *Last Light* to the subject of humor in my caregiving experience. I could have added the following episode.

We were standing in front of the cafeteria cashier, about to pay in advance for our lunch, when I sensed a large person just arriving to the back of my right shoulder. My wife drew back from my left side and said with a loud demanding tone, "What is that?" I turned to see the object of her query. He was a giant of a man—at least six foot-nine and built like a professional athlete.

Before I could regain control of Jane, she had placed herself toe to toe with the giant and, peering up into his face, again demanded, "What is that?" From up in the clouds came this reply, "Ho, ho—well, I guess I am kinda big."

"Alzheimer's!" I stammered, pulling Jane away. As soon as we were out of earshot, I gave her my lecture. "Jane, please pick on little, bitty men, not big ones." I glanced back to see if he really towered as high as he first appeared. He was every bit as tall as he seemed at first. So we put distance between us.

Injecting life and fun into a youth program seemed only the right thing to do. Boredom does not make young people more open to the Bible's teaching. Three of us young fellows still in seminary were invited to take charge of the activities and teaching of a summer Christian camp. We spread the word surreptitiously that the camp was about to be visited by Adolf Hitler, Superman, and a mad man. Meanwhile, I was busy designing our wardrobes and talking my two partners into helping with the scheme.

The one with straight black hair was ideal for Hitler. A broken black comb scotch-taped to his upper lip served as the mustache, and an old jacket with shoulder straps became his military dress. I posed as Superman in my sweat suit doctored up with all kinds of padding for huge muscles. Our pianist became the madman, dressed in his pajamas under a plastic raincoat, glasses cocked off the bridge of his nose, toothpaste frothing from his mouth.

Just as the campers were beginning to eat, we three burst into the dining room with a shout and the place erupted in laughter and excitement. The camp director seemed to appreciate our effort, and the week was indeed very productive in the lives of many of the young people.

More extreme measures seemed necessary for an old youth camp just being reopened deep in a rural area. The facility had been closed for a decade, and young people from surrounding farms lacked any real impact on their spiritual lives. Some of the churches had also closed.

Area pastors decided to repair and clean up the campgrounds and open it for a week of Bible teaching and recreation for young people of that region. And they came, filling the old camp to capacity. Again, three of us young men were invited to lead the camp.

But something seemed lacking—some spark of special fun that kids would remember and talk about, not to say the pastors. So I proposed a plan to my two fellow workers. Without being noticed, we posted ominous warnings on the trees around the dining hall: "Beware of the Black Death. It will strike some night soon!" Then we engaged the campers in conversation at the meal, asking them, "Whatever could those strange posted warnings mean?" Not even the pastors in charge had any clue.

On the appointed night we slipped from our quarters carrying firecrackers with specially prepared long fuses. These we planted on the porch of one of the cabins. Once they were lit, we went back to our quarters and stayed quiet until the explosions. As soon as things were again quiet, we slipped out through the darkness into an open area in the quiet woods that was central to all the cabins. Each of us then took our assigned position. I bellowed with all my strength in the mouth of a section of stovepipe serving as a megaphone: "The Black Death!" followed by my most hideous and threatening belly laugh.

Next, the big ex-marine stomped as hard as he could with his combat boots across the little wooden porch where the pastors were bunked. Then, at my signal, we all screamed as loud as we could in unison. Finally we departed quickly into the darkness and returned to our own quarters. The next morning as everyone gathered outside the mess hall for breakfast, the conversation indeed was lively. The stories of what each one heard were somewhat varied as each one vied to tell what happened just outside their door.

Beyond all of the excitement of the young campers was the concern of the pastors. I strolled over where they were standing in serious discussion, asking questions like, "Why would anyone want to fire guns among us? It must be some people from the other side of the lake who are angry to see the camp open again." Another one repeated his experience of terror, "It was awful! I sat bolt upright in my bunk, unable to move for fifteen minutes." Finally, the director stated that he would leave at once to contact the sheriff. At this, the three-man gospel team approached him in confession and repentance. We were the mysterious marauders. Then we stated frankly that the whole place and program needed stirring up. Before the week ended, practically every young person had made an open commitment to Jesus Christ. It seemed that they opened their hearts to us and our ministry all the more because of the excitement we had given them.

"Brighten the corner where you are" is the first line of a chorus I learned as a child in Sunday School. In recent years I have revived it, using an exaggerated version of an accent common in Rhode Island, where I now live. It has become one of my favorite pleasantries, especially when sung off-key—and accompanied by groans from my wife!

> Brighten the coanuh whe-uh you ah,
> Brighten the coanuh whe-uh you ah,
> Someone fah from hah-buh
> You may guide across the bah,
> Brighten the coanuh whe-uh you ahhh!

Of all my funny experiences, chasing a kidnapper, was undoubtedly the wildest. It all began early one morning about 2:00 A.M., when I was suddenly awakened by absolutely horrible screaming from two women not far from my house. From my upstairs bedroom window, I could see them just across the driveway on the side porch of my neighbor Jones. One was pounding on the door and screaming for Jones's help. The other was jumping about in terror and screaming. Both were in their pajamas. (Apparently the two women were sisters. The older sister lived a couple of doors down from our home, and the younger sister was spending the night with her. They were there alone with the older one's baby; both sisters were friends of my neighbor.)

"Wh-what is it?" called Jones from the window of his upstairs bedroom, which was just opposite mine.

"I saw a man in our home. We both ran out. The baby is still there. Oh, help us, PLEASE!!"

Instantly Jones was downstairs and out the door as the ladies led the way to the sidewalk. By this time, I was outside and hollered after Jones, "You got a gun?"

"No."

"I'll bring mine."

"Good!"

Here then is the scene. All are running single file down the sidewalk, with Jones in the lead, the older sister following him, then Jones's wife, then the more distraught younger sister. I was now charging across my front lawn with my .22 rifle, held at ready, just like I was taught in boot camp. The trouble was that only Jones knew that I was invited to the party.

Now the real excitement begins—when the younger woman catches a glimpse of me charging after her with gun in hand.

"Aieeee!" she screams, dancing up and down on the sidewalk. Other neighbors' shades are now popping up. At this precise moment a car swerves right at me and the screaming lady and screeches to a stop. From either side, out jump two off-duty policemen. (Mrs. Jones must have phoned the nearby station, catching the officers just as they were going out the door.) There I was with a gun and the lady screaming, so the young officer nearer me leaps at me, grabbing at the gun while yelling, "Police!"

Even now, I can recall the strange surge of competition that came over me. He was wrongfully trying to take my gun while I was on a mission of mercy! So around and around we go, hand over hand, each trying to get control of the rifle.

Just then Mrs. Jones looks around and cries out, "Nooo! You've got the minister!"

"OK, man, take it," I say, shoving the gun toward him, "but remember, it's loaded!"

By then, the other officer is standing utterly confused on the sidewalk near us, shaking his head and pleading, "Will someone please tell me what's going on here?" (They had come to catch a kidnapper and got the minister instead!)

Suddenly a more serious crisis comes to my mind. Jones by now is in the house, and the officer is charging up toward the door on the veranda with my loaded weapon. Sprinting toward the veranda, I discover that what I feared is happening: Jones is just emerging from the door, carrying a baby in his arms at the far end of the veranda, and the officer is racing at him with my gun. "Not that man either! He's my neighbor," I cry.

Immediately all of us pile into the house, generating a confusion worse than anything that had preceded. The officer in the house is chasing up and down the stairs, jumping around each corner trying to clear the place of any intruder. The young girl is whimpering and biting her lip, stumbling about the living room. Hoping to quiet her, I touch her elbow and say softly, "Things are OK, things are OK." Jerking herself around in wide-eyed horror, she points at me, screaming and shouting, "Here he is again!"

"Oh, keep still. You're going to be sick if you don't quiet yourself," I say a bit impatiently.

By now, other neighbors are crowding into the room. One large fellow with two German shepherds charges in—whether to attack or to rescue, I'm not sure.

As for the kidnapper, I feel he either escaped early on or by now, or he would be a victim of heart failure amid all this disruption. The more likely explanation is that a broom fell over on the stairs and started the ball of all these coincidences rolling.

In utter amazement I walked back to my front door and found Jane waiting with the question I expected but dreaded, "What happened?"

"You'll never believe what I'm about to tell you." With that, we sat in bed until nearly dawn, laughing and recounting each part of this complex episode. The next day we scoured the newspapers, wondering how such an episode would be published. Apparently, no one wanted to see the story in print—not the two women, not the police, not Jones, not the minister. At a later date Jane and I met with the Joneses over coffee to see if it all could have been our imagination, but our accounts agreed exactly. And finally now, for the first time, I have made public the detail of this adventure, my funniest escapade.

www.ingramcontent.com/pod-product-compliance
Lightning Source LLC
Chambersburg PA
CBHW071531040426
42452CB00008B/975